THE IMPORTANCE OF

Sir Isaac Newton

These and other titles are included in The Importance Of biography series:

Alexander the Great
Napoleon Bonaparte
Cleopatra
Christopher Columbus
Marie Curie
Thomas Edison
Albert Einstein
Benjamin Franklin
Galileo Galilei
Jim Henson
Thomas Jefferson
Chief Joseph
Malcolm X

Margaret Mead
Michelangelo
Wolfgang Amadeus Mozart
Sir Isaac Newton
Richard M. Nixon
Jackie Robinson
Anwar Sadat
Margaret Sanger
John Steinbeck
Jim Thorpe
Mark Twain
H.G. Wells

THE IMPORTANCE OF

Sir
Isaac Newton

by
**Deborah Hitzeroth and
Sharon Leon**

Lucent Books, P.O. Box 289011, San Diego, CA 92198-9011

Library of Congress Cataloging-in-Publication Data

Hitzeroth, Deborah, 1961-
    Isaac Newton / by Deborah Hitzeroth and Sharon Leon.
       p. cm.—(The Importance Of)
    Includes bibliographical references and index.
    ISBN 1-56006-046-8 (alk. paper)
    1. Newton, Isaac, Sir 1642-1727—Juvenile literature.
2. Physicists—Great Britain—Biography—Juvenile literature.
[1. Newton, Isaac, Sir 1642-1727. 2. Scientists.]   I. Leon,
Sharon, 1959- . II. Title. II. Series
QC16.N7H52   1994
530'.912—dc20
[B]   93-38680
                                          CIP
                                           AC

Copyright 1994 by Lucent Books, Inc., P.O. Box 289011,
San Diego, California, 92198-9011

Printed in the U.S.A.

Contents

Foreword

THE IMPORTANCE OF biography series deals with individuals who have made a unique contribution to history. The editors of the series have deliberately chosen to cast a wide net and include people from all fields of endeavor. Individuals from politics, music, art, literature, philosophy, science, sports, and religion are all represented. In addition, the editors did not restrict the series to individuals whose accomplishments have helped change the course of history. Of necessity, this criterion would have eliminated many whose contribution was great, though limited. Charles Darwin, for example, was responsible for radically altering the scientific view of the natural history of the world. His achievements continue to impact the study of science today. Others, such as Chief Joseph of the Nez Percé, played a pivotal role in the history of their own people. While Joseph's influence does not extend much beyond the Nez Percé, his nonviolent resistance to white expansion and his continuing role in protecting his tribe and his homeland remain an inspiration to all.

These biographies are more than factual chronicles. Each volume attempts to emphasize an individual's contributions both in his or her own time and for posterity. For example, the voyages of Christopher Columbus opened the way to European colonization of the New World. Unquestionably, his encounter with the New World brought monumental changes to both Europe and the Americas in his day. Today, however, the broader impact of Columbus's voyages is being critically scrutinized. *Christopher Columbus,* as well as every biography in The Importance Of series, includes and evaluates the most recent scholarship available on each subject.

Each author includes a wide variety of primary and secondary source quotations to document and substantiate his or her work. All quotes are footnoted to show readers exactly how and where biographers derive their information, as well as to provide stepping stones to further research. These quotations enliven the text by giving readers eyewitness views of the life and times of each individual covered in The Importance Of series.

Finally, each volume is enhanced by photographs, bibliographies, chronologies, and comprehensive indexes. For both the casual reader and the student engaged in research, The Importance Of biographies will be a fascinating adventure into the lives of people who have helped shape humanity's past and present, and who will continue to shape its future.

Important Dates in the Life of Sir Isaac Newton

Isaac Newton is born on December 25 in Woolsthorpe, England. — **1642**

1646

Begins school. — **1647**

┌ Mother, Hannah, marries Reverend Barnabas Smith; Newton continues to live at Woolsthorpe with his grandmother.

1654 ┌ Enrolls in school at Grantham and moves in with the Clarke family.

Leaves Grantham to help on the family farm. — **1658**

1660 ┐ Enrolls at Cambridge University to pursue the life of a scholar.

Buys his first prism and begins experiments on the nature of light. — **1664**

1665-1667 ┐ Flees the plague in London and returns to Woolsthorpe; lays the groundwork for his universal theory of gravity, the composition of light, and calculus.

Returns to Cambridge and wins academic acclaim; becomes a minor fellow. — **1667**

1669 — Appointed Lucasian Professor of Mathematics; produces first paper on calculus.

Makes reflecting telescope and presents it to the Royal Society. ┌ **1671**

1672 ┐ Elected a member of the Royal Society, a prestigious scientific fellowship; sends first paper on the composition of light to the society; enters into public controversy over his paper.

Mentor Isaac Barrow dies. — **1677**

1678

Mother Hannah dies. ┐ **1679**

John Collins, a prominent member of the Royal Society and Newton's friend, dies. └ **1683**

┐ Henry Oldenburg, secretary of the Royal Society and Newton's longtime correspondent, dies.

1684

Astronomer Edmond Halley visits Newton and poses questions which lead Newton to write the *Principia*. ┘ **1687**

┐ Newton publishes the *Principia*, a manuscript consisting of three books outlining the laws of motion, gravitation, and hydrodynamics.

Has nervous breakdown. ┘ **1692**

1696 ┐ Becomes warden of the mint.

Becomes master of the mint and completes recoinage of English monetary system. — **1699**

1703 — Elected president of the Royal Society; longtime foe Robert Hooke dies and Newton feels free to publish his work on optics.

1704

Publishes *Optics*. ┘ **1705**

┐ Knighted by Queen Anne; first time in history a scientist receives this honor.

Dies on March 20, 1727; buried in Westminster Abbey. — **1727**

A Sharper Eye

In the history of science, Sir Isaac Newton stands out as one of the world's most important figures. Inventor, scholar, and researcher, Newton formulated the basis of all modern science.

In his greatest work, *Mathematical Principles of Natural Philosophy* or *Principia*, Newton created the framework for physics, developed the laws of motion, and outlined the laws of universal gravitation. According to historian Bernard Cohen, Newton's writings fostered "one of the most profound revolutions in the history of human thought."[1]

An Unceasing Curiosity

Newton's unceasing curiosity and study of the world around him contributed to his success. He sat in his mother's orchard one day and watched an apple fall from a tree. Another man might have seen just an apple; Newton saw a universal mystery. From that moment, he tirelessly sought to discover the nature of the mysterious force that caused the apple's fall and its effect on the universe. From his curious musings in the garden, Newton developed a theory that explained one of the most basic laws of the universe—the law of gravity. And Newton's theories are as important to us today as they were to scientists during his own time. Newton's theories of gravity, light, and motion are still used today in radios, television, space shuttles, and telescopes.

Newton's discoveries have earned him an almost mythic place in scientific history.

With keen observation and unceasing curiosity, Newton often pondered the forces of nature. To the thoughtful Newton, even a falling apple represented a universal mystery.

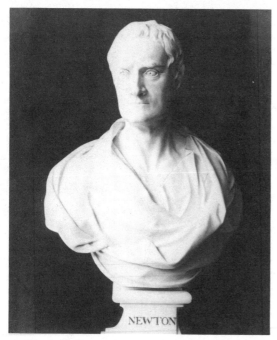

At Cambridge University a bust of Newton depicts the revered scientist as a Greek god. It serves as a reminder of the great man who once roamed the university halls as a student and later as a professor.

During his life, Newton was honored by the scientific community; after his death, he was revered as nearly superhuman. His fame and reputation continue to live long after his death. In the three centuries since his great discoveries, nearly every grade school student in the world has come to know Newton's name.

Newton once said that if he saw farther than other men, it was because he stood on the shoulders of giants—the scientists who came before him and laid the groundwork for his dazzling theories. Newton's work summed up the work of all his predecessors: Copernicus, Galileo, and Kepler. He built upon their work and took it further than even they could have imagined. Those who came afterward acknowledged that Newton had a keenness of sight that was unequaled in history. If he saw farther than those before him, it was because he examined everything with a sharper eye.

1 The Birth of a Genius

When Isaac Newton was born in Woolsthorpe, England, on Christmas Day 1642, little revealed that this tiny, weak infant would someday become one of the most revered scientists of all time. Very premature and given little hope of survival, Newton was so small at birth that he could have slept in a one-quart pot. Even the two family servants, who were sent to a nearby house for some home-brewed medicine, doubted that he would live more than a few hours. Instead of rushing to the neighbor's house, they "sate down on a stile by the way" because "there was no [reason] for making haste, for they were sure the child would be dead before they could get back."[2]

An engraving of the room in which Isaac Newton was born. At birth, Newton was weak, with little hope of survival. No one could have predicted the important scientific contributions that he would one day make.

A Lonely Childhood

In addition to being small and weak, Isaac carried the burden of growing up almost alone. Newton never met his father, a farmer also named Isaac, who died around two months before his son was born. No one knows the cause of the senior Newton's early death at the age of thirty-six. Three years later, Newton's mother, Hannah Ayscough, also withdrew from his life. Hannah had been married only six months when Isaac's father died and left her a widow at age twenty-five. Being so young, she was expected to marry again. With the help of her brother, a local minister, Hannah soon found a new husband. On January 27, 1646, she wed Reverend Barnabas Smith, a man more than thirty years her senior. Following the wedding, she moved to Smith's church in North Hampton, a small village a mile south of Woolsthorpe, while Isaac remained at the family farm with his grandmother.

Hannah feared that moving her son from the family farm would endanger his title to the land. Though the Newtons' farm was relatively small and produced little income for the family, it was an important possession. Whoever owned the manor, comprised of a small house, three small farms, and a few thatched cottages, would inherit the desirable social title of Lord of the Manor. The three-year-old could not fully understand his mother's plan for his future. He felt abandoned by his mother and developed a disdain for his stepfather. In a list of sins that Newton compiled as a teenager, he revealed these and other feelings, including "threatening my father and mother Smith to burne them and the house over them."[3]

Though Newton's mother's remarriage took her away from her son, it also opened the doors of education to him. Hannah

Newton spent many lonely childhood years at Woolsthorpe Manor under the care of his grandmother.

At the age of twelve Newton went to live with a family in Grantham so that he could continue his education. Unlike rural Woolsthorpe, Grantham was a bustling town with plenty of activities to occupy young Isaac.

had originally come from a poor but well-educated family. Newton's biological father, a farmer, was not interested in education. If Newton's father had lived, it is likely that Newton would never have attended school. In contrast, Reverend Smith was well educated (he had a master's degree from Oxford) and was wealthy enough to send his stepson to school. Despite his lack of interest in the boy, Reverend Smith believed education was important. So, with his mother's and stepfather's support, Newton began school in 1647.

School Time

Newton received his early education at two small, one-room schoolhouses near home. They were located in Skillington and Stoke Rochford, villages within walking distance of Woolsthorpe. Not much is known about Newton's life during this period. No school records remain and New-ton kept no notes on his studies. The few details about his life at this time paint the picture of a lonely young boy growing up in isolation. With only his grandmother and a few servants as company, Newton spent most of his time alone. Newton's secluded life continued for eight years. Then, the year Isaac turned eleven, Reverend Smith died and Hannah returned to Woolsthorpe to live, bringing along her three other children, Benjamin, Mary, and Hannah Smith. Suddenly the quiet house was filled with people and noise. Newton had his mother back again, but he was not able to enjoy his new family for long. When Newton turned twelve in 1654, Hannah decided it was time to expand her son's education. She enrolled him at the Free Grammar School in Grantham, a town about seven miles from Woolsthorpe. The distance was too far to walk each day, so Hannah arranged for Newton to live with a family in Grantham. Hannah chose the Clarke family, whom she had known since childhood, to care for her son.

From the Country to the City

Life in Grantham was very different from life on the farm. Grantham was a bustling town filled with activity. In the active city, Isaac began to develop his mechanical and mathematical talents and his interest in experiments. One account of Newton's days in Grantham reveals his fascination with a windmill's construction. Waterwheels on the area's rivers generated much of the village's power, and the windmill was a curiosity. Every morning before school, Isaac would rush to the windmill's construction site and loiter near the carpenters on his way home at night. As he watched the tower slowly grow, Newton

A wash drawing depicts Newton experimenting with his water clock. As a boy, Newton was fascinated by mechanical devices.

became convinced he could build one himself. As he did with many of his later projects, Newton started this enterprise in secret. A few mornings after beginning his undercover project, he unveiled his invention to the Clarke family after breakfast. Newton had attached a miniature windmill to the steep roof of their house, and from the street below the Clarkes could see the mill spinning wildly in the wind. This was one of Newton's first major projects, and its success sparked his interest in building other scientific instruments.

A Timely Invention

In addition to windmills, clocks and sundials also fascinated Newton. In the seventeenth century, clocks were a luxury only the rich could afford. Isaac decided to build his own. His early inventions were simple but accurate sundials, made by drilling pegs into the walls of a house and marking the length and directions of their shadows throughout the day. After careful observation, Newton was able to draw a circle around the pegs so that they could be used as an accurate sundial. He made a huge sundial on the side of the Clarkes' house in Grantham and also made several at Woolsthorpe for his own family. Two of his early sundials still exist at Woolsthorpe and are on view for tourists.

Carrying his experiments further, Newton next built a water clock. This device, called a clepsydra, was well known during Newton's time. The clepsydra looked much like a modern clock from the outside. The instrument was a four-foot-tall box with the hours marked on a dial at the top. This type of clock had only

Newton demonstrates his model windmill to friends. In Grantham, Newton became somewhat of a celebrity for his many inventions.

strange inventions, and extraordinary inclination for mechanics . . . [and how] instead of playing among the other boys . . . he always busied himself making knick-knacks and models of wood in many kinds. For which purpose he had got little saws, hatchets, hammers, and all sorts of tools, which he would use with great dexterity.[5]

A Dreamer of Dreams

Unfortunately, Newton showed none of his genius at school, where he was known as an indifferent student. Newton ranked at the bottom of his class, and he had a reputation as a daydreamer. During this time, students' desks were arranged according to their academic performance. The best students sat in the front of the room, and the worst sat in back. Newton's desk was always in the back. While the other students recited lessons or answered questions, Newton would stare out the window and dream. His teachers doubted that he would ever be a successful scholar.

Summarizing conversations with the scientist, Stukeley wrote of Newton's school years:

[Newton's] fancies sometimes engrossed so much of his thoughts, that he was apt to neglect his book, and dull boys were . . . put over him in [class]. . . . Still nothing could induce him to lay by his mechanical experiments: but all holidays, and what time the boys [were] allowed to play, he spent entirely in knocking and hammering in his lodging room, pursuing that strong bent of his . . . not only in things serious, but ludicrous too.[6]

an hour hand because minute hands were not used during Newton's time. Inside the clock, water dripped slowly from one container to another. As the bottom container filled, the rising water slowly pushed up a wooden float. The float was attached to the hour hand, and as it rose, it turned the hands of the clock. According to Newton's first biographer, Dr. William Stukeley, this clock was a great success and "stood in the room where he lay, and [Newton] took care every morning to supply it with its proper quantity of water. And the family upon occasion would go to see what was the hour by it, and it was left in the house long after he went away."[4]

According to Stukeley, people all over town talked about Newton and his

A Handy Young Man

Even as a young boy, Newton was an avid inventor. In Frank E. Manuel's A Portrait of Isaac Newton, *Dr. William Stukeley, one of Newton's earliest biographers, describes a water clock Newton invented.*

"Sir Isaac's water clock is much talked of. This he made out of a box he begged of [his landlord's] wife's brother. . . . It resembled pretty much our common clocks and clock-cases, but less; for it was not above four feet in height. . . . There was a dial plate at top with figures of the hours. The index was turned by a piece of wood, which either fell or rose by water dropping. This stood in the room where he [slept], and he took care every morning to supply it with its proper quantity of water; and the family upon occasion would go to see what was the hour by it. It was left in the house long after he went away to the University. . . . These fancies sometimes engrossed so much of his thoughts, that he was apt to neglect his book, and dull boys were now and then put over him in [school]."

One of the frivolous inventions to which Newton devoted his time was creating scary kites. Kite flying was a favorite pastime of children at the time, and Newton enjoyed the sport along with the other boys in town. On warm nights, the boys would go to a field on the edge of town and fly their kites until it was too dark to see. Not content with the simple kites most of the boys used, Newton built small lanterns which he attached to the tail of his kite. As the sun set, light from the candles inside the lanterns could be seen for miles. At a distance, it looked like the lights were floating in the air all by themselves. When the lights first appeared, the townspeople were terrified. Many were convinced that ghosts or demons caused the lights. Upon investigation, the townspeople found the lights were simply another of young Newton's strange creations.

A New Challenge

Newton was always quick to apply himself to a challenge and it was such a challenge that helped Newton excel at school. He changed his attitude toward school not to please his teachers, however, but to attain revenge. As Newton walked to class one day, the school bully attacked him. Following the beating, Newton limped to school in pain, already planning his revenge. Later that morning, Newton challenged his attacker to a rematch after class. According to historian John Conduitt, when school was over the two boys went into the . . . yard. While they were fighting, the [teacher's] son came out, and encouraged them by clapping one on the back, and winking at the other. Isaac Newton had the more spirit and resolution, and beat [the bully] till he would fight no more. Young Stokes [the schoolmaster's son] told Isaac Newton to treat [his opponent] like a coward and rub his nose against the wall, and accordingly Isaac . . . pulled him along by the ears and thrust his face against the side of the church.[7]

As his schoolmates watched, the class dreamer beat his opponent and then scraped the boy's nose across the school-yard fence. Winning the fight was not enough for Newton though, and he began to plan another type of revenge. The bully was ranked higher than Newton in school, and Newton was determined to beat him in the classroom as well. To the amazement of his teacher, Newton was soon the best student in school with a front-row seat in class. According to Stukeley, Newton became one of his teacher's favorite pupils. At one point the teacher, Henry Stokes,

Determined to outrank the school bully, Newton quickly transformed himself from the class daydreamer to the best student at Grantham Grammar School.

Gale E. Christianson's book, In the Presence of the Creator, *quotes Newton's friend Catherine Storey on how Newton preferred experimenting to playing games with the other boys.*

"Isaac was always a sober, silent, thinking lad and never was known to play with the boys . . . at their silly amusements, but would rather chuse to be at home even among the girls, and would frequently make little tables, cupboards, and other utensils for [Miss Storey] and her [friends], to set their [dolls] and trinkets on. . . . Likewise [he made] a cart with four wheels wherein he would fit, and by turning a [crank] about he could make it carry him around the house wither he pleased."

"with the pride of a father put [Newton] in the most conspicuous place of the school and with tears in his eyes made a speech in his praise to excite the boys to follow his example."[8] Perhaps Newton did have a future as a scholar. But Newton's life changed before he could embark on a scholarly future. In 1658 when he was seventeen, his mother decided it was time for him to return home and learn to manage the farm.

An Absentminded Farmer

Newton returned home, but he was not happy. His mother's plan to make him a farmer proved a complete failure. Newton's interests lay more in books and building mechanical toys than in farming.

Many stories are told of Newton and his absentmindedness during this time. If Newton was sent to watch the sheep graze, he would wander away to read and the sheep would wander into the crops. If he

was sent to town on horseback, he sometimes came back on foot. As Lord of the Manor, Newton attended to business in Grantham. On the way, a steep hill outside of town forced riders to dismount and lead their horses up the hill. One day, Newton forgot to remount his horse and walked the remainder of the way into town. Another time, Newton's horse slipped away while he was not paying attention. Newton did not notice the horse's absence until he reached the top of the hill.

One day Newton's uncle, William Ayscough, suspicious that Newton was idling away his time instead of learning the family business, followed Newton into town. As he suspected, he found Newton reading under a hedge while the family servant conducted the business. In frustration he said, "Go back to your studies, Isaac, either you're a great loafer or a great genius—the Lord alone knows which."[9]

Newton's uncle was not the only person who thought Newton should be studying instead of farming. Newton's former teacher, Master Stokes, asked Hannah to send her son back to school. According to Stukeley,

> Mr. Stokes, who had a great value for [Newton], often strongly solicited his mother to return him to his learning, the proper channel of [Newton's desires]. [Stokes] told her it was a great loss to the world as well as a vain attempt to bury so promising a genius in rustic employment, which was . . . opposite to his temper; . . . that the only way whereby he could either preserve or raise his fortune must be by fitting [Newton] for the University.[10]

Finally, much to the relief of the servants who thought their new lord was a fool, Hannah gave in to Stokes's suggestion and sent Newton to the University of Cambridge in 1660.

On to Cambridge

Up to this time, Newton had received what was considered a standard education. He had studied Greek and Latin classics and a little Hebrew, ancient history, biblical history, and grammar. When he left for the university, he knew little math beyond basic addition, subtraction, multiplication, and division. This would not hinder his progress at Cambridge, though, because the school's approach was far from rigorously scientific. Philosophical and theological study were still the chief academic fields. The relatively new and radical ideas of Galileo and Kepler had not yet penetrated the halls of English universities.

Academically, England lagged far behind the universities of Italy and France,

At the suggestion of a former teacher who recognized Newton's potential, Newton was enrolled in the University of Cambridge in 1660.

and the structure of English universities helped contribute to the country's poor scholarly reputation. University rules required that each student be assigned to a tutor, who oversaw most of the student's education. University professors, called fellows of the university, were required to give a minimum number of lectures each year. But students were not required to attend any of these lectures. If students did attend a lecture series, they usually had no time to question the lecturing professor. If students had questions, or disagreed with what they had heard, they could meet with the professor privately, if the professor agreed. More commonly, students would take their questions or arguments back to their tutors for discussion. The tutor's job was to recommend books and papers for the student to read, recommend lectures to attend, conduct classes, and also act as a substitute parent. The system's major weakness was that it assumed that one tutor could provide all the instruction a student needed in every subject. This was usually impossible.

Cambridge mathematician John Wallis, a founding member of the English Royal Society (a group dedicated to promoting scientific learning) described his experience of the typical university education of the time:

> I had none to direct me, what books to read, or what to seek, or in which method to proceed. . . . And amongst more than two hundred students (at that time) in our college, I do not know of any two . . . who had more mathematics than I . . . which was but little.[11]

Newton was assigned to Benjamin Pulleyn, a professor of Greek studies at the university. Little is known of Pulleyn, and Newton never wrote of his relationship

The School of Pythagoras at Cambridge, named after the Greek philosopher and mathematician. With philosophy and theology the chief fields of study at Cambridge, the students received little mathematical training.

Building Habits for Life

Newton's early practice of experimenting and building mechanical devices established lifelong habits. In a passage from Frank E. Manuel's A Portrait of Isaac Newton, *Dr. William Stukeley outlines how Newton's youthful activities helped him make his later scientific discoveries.*

"It seems to me . . . that Sir Isaac's early use and expertness at his mechanical tools, and his faculty of drawing and designing, were of service to him, in his experimental way of [science]; and prepar'd for him a solid foundation to exercise his strong reasoning facultys upon; his . . . discernment of causes and effects, . . . his profound judgment, his . . . perseverance in finding out his solutions and demonstrations, and in his experiments; his vast strength of mind . . . ; his . . . attachment to calculations; . . . all these united in one man, and that in an extraordinary degree. . . . [His] mechanical knack, and skill in drawing, very much assist[ed] in making experiments. . . . For want of this handycraft, how many philosophers quietly sit in their [libraries] and invent an *hypothesis*; but Sir Isaac's way was by dint of experiments to [prove his ideas]."

with his earliest college teacher. Pulleyn, however, was considered a "pupil monger," or a professor who took a large number of students to expand his income. Most professors received an extra stipend for each student they tutored. When Newton came to Cambridge, more than fifty students were already assigned to Pulleyn. There is little evidence that Newton's first teacher spent much time with him.

An Inquisitive Mind

But Newton was determined to learn everything he could while at Cambridge. What Newton did not receive from his professor or tutor, he resolved to learn for himself. He attended lectures on a wide range of subjects and sought professors to teach him. In his university bedroom, Newton built his own laboratory. Although he made no great discoveries in his early years at Cambridge, he established a lifelong habit of experimentation.While at Cambridge, Newton met Isaac Barrow, who greatly influenced him. Newton began taking lessons in natural history and optics from Barrow and became intrigued with mathematics. Under Barrow's direction, Newton read Euclid's geometry and learned trigonometry. Newton also learned about the Copernican system of astronomy. This system, named after Nicolaus Copernicus, the Polish priest who developed the theory, states that the sun is the center of the universe and that all the planets rotate around the sun. Prior to Copernicus's writings, most people believed that the sun and planets revolved around the earth. Copernicus published his theories in 1543, and they remained controversial, even though they were proven true by the Italian scientist Galileo Galilei during the early 1600s. While Copernicus's ideas were spreading, many people still opposed his theories and his ideas were not widely taught at English universities. In addition to reading Copernicus's writings, Newton also read Kepler's *Optics*. The works of Copernicus, Galileo, and Kepler sparked Newton's interest in telescopes and light. During this time, Newton also began to compile notebooks of his observations on light refraction, lens grinding, and mathematical problems that fascinated him.

Johannes Kepler's Optics *sparked Newton's interest in telescopes and light.*

Intrigued by mathematics, Newton read the writings of Nicolaus Copernicus (pictured), whose theories about the universe were considered too controversial for English universities.

Though Newton was eager to learn, his financial situation constrained his experiments and self-education. Although Newton's mother had the money to pay for his education, she felt there was no reason to pay for what Newton could earn on his own. So Newton attended the university as a *subsizar*, a student who worked to pay for his education. He paid his tuition and living expenses by running errands, working in the kitchen, and waiting on his tutor, and squeezed his study time in between his work hours.

Even with the added burden of working as a *subsizar*, Newton was able to earn his bachelor's degree in January 1665. Still hungry for knowledge, Newton was eager to continue his education. But his academic plans were cut short when the Great Plague struck England that spring, forcing Newton to flee London for the seclusion and safety of Woolsthorpe.

2 The Seeds of Genius

Throughout his life, Newton felt that he was divinely blessed and destined to perform great deeds. In his later years, Newton attributed both his miraculous survival as an infant and his escape from the plague to this destiny. Whether destiny or luck were responsible, Newton was indeed fortunate to escape death by the plague. The disease was fast and deadly, quickly spreading from a few cases to epidemic proportions in a period of only a few weeks. The journal entries of Samuel Pepys, a secretary of the British admiralty, show how quickly the malady spread. On April 30, 1665, wrote Pepys, "[there are] great fears of the Sickenesse here in the city, it being said that two or three houses are already shut up. God preserve us all." Within two months the disease was so widespread that Pepys wrote that he had resolved "to put all [his] affairs in the world in good order, the season growing so sickly that it is much to be feared how a man can [escape the disease]."[12]

The Great Plague of London

More than 90 percent of those struck by the disease died. By September 1665, when the Great Plague reached its peak,

eight thousand people were dying each week in the city of London alone. The only effective way of surviving the epidemic was to follow the advice of a fourteenth-century

Newton believed that destiny spared him from death during the Great Plague of London, which claimed over a hundred thousand lives.

remedy: *cito, longe, tarde* (fly quickly, go far, return slowly). Unfortunately, many tarried inside the city too long and became infected with the plague before they left. When they fled the city, they carried the disease with them and spread the plague into the surrounding countryside. The plague eventually entered the halls of Cambridge University. By August 1665, all public meetings at Cambridge were prohibited and faculty members and students were sent away from the college.

Fleeing the City

When the university closed in the summer of 1665, Newton left Cambridge for the secluded countryside of Lincolnshire. Isolated from the bustle of college life, Newton was safe from the dangers of the plague-ridden city. The isolation also gave him many solitary hours to think about what he had learned at the university. At Cambridge, Newton never had time to fully explore his theories due to his hectic school schedule. In the peace of his family manor, Newton contemplated all that he learned at Cambridge and expanded on it. The two years he spent in the quiet countryside of Lincolnshire proved to be the most creative of his entire life. Newton biographer Derek T. Whiteside wrote that by

> mid-1665, . . . the urge to learn from the work of others was largely abated. . . . It was time for him to go his own way in earnest and thereafter, though he continued to draw in detail on the ideas of others, Newton took his real inspiration from the workings of his own fertile mind.[13]

During this time, Newton became completely immersed in his work. His papers from this period "throb with energy and imagination but yet convey the claustrophobic air of a man completely wrapped up in himself, whose only real contact with the external world was through his books."[14]

Newton himself felt that the years 1665-1666 were the most inventive of his life. Shortly before his death, he wrote to

To escape the plague, Newton fled to the secluded countryside of Lincolnshire, where he immersed himself in work.

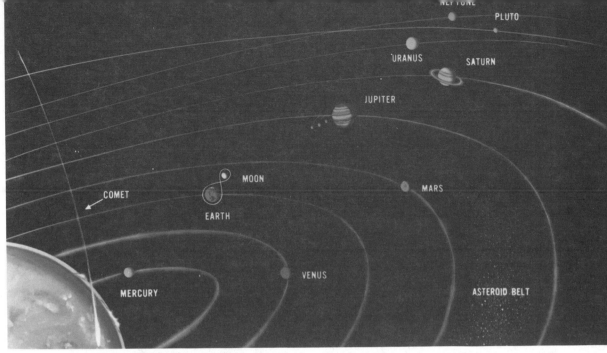

Galileo and Copernicus proved that the earth and the planets were moving bodies. Inspired by their work, Newton developed a mathematical method that could accurately measure bodies in motion.

the Huguenot scholar Pierre des Maizeaux concerning his months at Woolsthorpe.

> In the beginning of the year 1665, I found the Method of [calculus] . . . and the next year in January had the Theory of Colours and . . . the same year I began to think of gravity . . . [and] deduced . . . the forces which keep the Planets in their Orbs. . . . All this was in the two plague years of 1665 and 1666. For in those days I was in the prime of my age of invention and minded Mathematics and Philosophy more than at any time since.[15]

Calculus

One of the first problems Newton wanted to solve was how to measure bodies in mo-

tion accurately. The works of Galileo and Copernicus had focused science's attention on the field of motion. Once the earth and other planets were proven to be moving bodies, scientists wanted to measure and study the nature of this movement. At the time, no easy way existed to measure the speed nor calculate the changing position of a moving body, especially one that varied speed and direction as it traveled. Other scientists had been searching for a way to measure the accelerations, velocities, and distances traveled by moving bodies. Newton found a new mathematical method which could be used to quickly compute the answers to all these problems.

Newton called his mathematical method "fluxions," based on the Latin word *fluxio* meaning "flowing or changing." Today we call this type of math calculus. Calculus is based on the idea that a body in motion does not travel in a definite and unchanging way; instead, its speed constantly changes and eventually lessens. Today calculus is used to predict the orbit of satellites, calculate the changes of acceleration in an object falling through space, and compute the arc of a revolving planet.

Newton composed his first major paper on mathematics at Cambridge in May 1665, shortly before leaving London. Newton's ideas in the paper, which dealt with measuring the arcs of curves, would later blossom into his theory of fluxions at Woolsthorpe.

The Theory of Fluxions

Newton's theory was fairly simple, but it formed the basis of the entire system of fluxions. Newton's theory stated that the path of a moving object should not be thought of as a series of points, but as a single, continually moving point. Newton developed a new set of symbols which could be used in mathematical equations to denote a moving object. From this very basic beginning, the theory of fluxions developed. Newton wrote several short papers on his theory, but did not publish them. Newton knew the ideas of a young scientist with only a bachelor's degree would receive little attention. Instead of sharing his ideas with the world, Newton put his papers away for later publication, when he was older and had established a scholarly reputation. Once he completed his initial work on fluxions, Newton turned his attention in a new direction—to the mystery of gravity.

The ancient Greek philosopher Aristotle used the term gravity simply to mean heaviness. It was not until the sixteenth century that his theories were disproven.

Until the seventeenth century, no one was sure what force pulled some objects, like rocks, toward the ground. Scientists also wondered why the sun and stars floated in the sky and what kept the planets in orbit around the sun. While Newton was in school, most universities still presented the scientific theories of the ancient Greek philosopher Aristotle. Aristotle believed that all objects were driven by some inner impulse to seek their natural places in the universe. Aristotelians, those who followed Aristotle's teachings, believed that this was the reason things fell to the ground.

Aristotelians used the term gravity simply to mean heaviness. The more heaviness or gravity an object had, the more quickly it would fall to earth. According to this theory, objects with little heaviness, like fire, sought the sky. Objects with great heaviness, like rocks, sought the ground.

Aristotle's ideas held for thousands of years until the scientific revolution began chipping away at them. During the sixteenth century, Italian scientist Galileo Galilei developed a startling new idea. His experiments seemed to prove that all objects, no matter how heavy, fell at the same rate of speed. Galileo stated that if air resistance could be eliminated, then a feather would fall as fast as an iron ball. This was a direct contradiction of Aristotle's teaching. Galileo's theories inspired scientists to try to discover the force that pulled

Galileo Galilei proved that all objects, no matter how heavy, fall at the same rate of speed. His experiments shattered the Aristotelian theories about gravity.

the objects toward the ground. Like the Aristotelians, scientists called this force gravity. While some scientists worked on the riddle of gravity, other scientists tried to solve the puzzle of how and why planets rotated around the sun.

Italian scientist Giovanni Borelli, whose work was published in the mid-1600s, theorized that two forces might be acting on a planet during its travel through space. Borelli imagined a universe where one force pulled the planets toward the sun while another dragged them out toward space. Borelli believed the power pulling the planets away from the sun was centrifugal force. An object that moves in a circular motion will be pulled away from the center of the circle by centrifugal force. Robert Hooke, a noted English scientist and Newton's chief rival in later years, also tried to prove a similar theory through experimentation. While Borelli and Hooke's ideas were on the right track, they both lacked the mathematical skills necessary to prove their ideas. It was Newton, a young unknown scholar, who finally linked the two conflicting forces and developed a new system of how the universe operates.

A Simple Apple: Key to the Universe

Newton said that a simple apple helped him solve the mystery of what held the universe together. The French philosopher Voltaire wrote about Newton's discovery in his *Element de la Philosophie de Newton*: "One day in the year 1666, Newton, having returned to the country and seeing the fruits of a tree fall, fell . . . into

Newton's Apple

Biographer Henry Pemberton describes how Newton developed his theory on universal gravitation. The following excerpt is taken from Gale E. Christianson's In the Presence of the Creator.

"As he sat alone in a garden, he fell into speculation on the power of gravity: that as this power is not found . . . diminished at the remotest distance from the center of the earth, to which we can rise, neither at the tops of the loftiest buildings, nor even on the summits of the highest mountains; it appeared to him reasonable to conclude, that this power must extend much farther than was usually thought; why not as high as the moon . . . and if so, her motion must be influenced by it; perhaps she is retained in her orbit thereby. . . . He considered with himself, that if the moon be retained in her orbit by force of gravity, no doubt the primary planets are carried round the sun by the like power. And by comparing the periods of the several planets with their distances from the sun, he found, that if any power like gravity held them in their courses its strength must decrease in the . . . proportion of the increase of the distance."

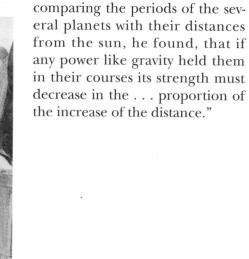

Newton ponders the mystery of the force that causes an apple to fall to the ground.

a deep meditation about the cause that thus attracts all bodies [toward earth]."[16]

Newton watched the apple fall to the ground and wondered about the force that pulled it downward. Was it the same force that kept him firmly anchored to the ground? And if so, how far above the earth did it extend? Did it go as far as the highest mountaintop, or did it go farther still? Perhaps the force extended as far as the moon. If so, then perhaps this same force that pulled the apple toward the ground kept the moon in rotation around the earth and the planets in rotation around the sun. Newton theorized that the centrifugal force of the moon spinning around the earth would be counterbalanced by the force of gravity pulling it toward earth. The pull of the earth's force was weak enough to keep the moon from being pulled in and crashing into the earth, but strong enough to keep the moon from spinning away into space. Newton thought perhaps this force worked not only on earth, but throughout the universe. Newton wrote in his journal: "In . . . (1666) I began to think of gravity extending to the orb of the moon, and . . . I deduced . . . the forces which keep the planets in their orbs."[17] Newton would later develop these basic ideas into the universal laws of motion and gravitation. Newton put aside this theory, too, and began delving into other scientific mysteries.

Seeing the Light

The forces that pulled Newton away from his scientific pondering, however, were his experiments. Since his youth, Newton had been addicted to experimentation to probe nature's mysteries. One mystery Newton wanted to solve was the composition and nature of light. Like many other scientists at the time, Newton experimented with prisms and lenses to see how they refracted light. Refraction is the bending of a ray of light when it passes from the air through a piece of glass.

Italian scientist Galileo Galilei sparked this interest by making astonishing discoveries with handmade refracting telescopes during the 1600s. With his relatively weak telescopes, Galileo found mountains on the moon and moons around the planet

Galileo used this telescope to locate the moons around Jupiter and the mountains on the earth's moon. These discoveries provided evidence that the earth revolved around the sun.

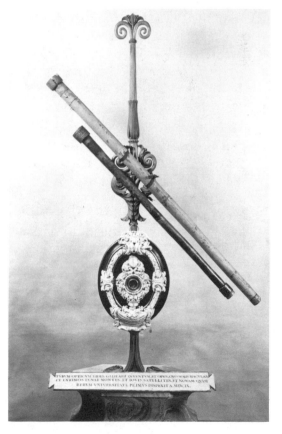

Jupiter, and provided evidence that the earth revolved around the sun. These early telescopes were fitted with lenses on both ends. The lens on the front end, called the objective lens, bent or refracted light as it entered the telescope. The lens bent the light so that all the light rays gathered by the scope were focused at one point in the telescope tube. This process produced an image inside the telescope. This image was then magnified by the eyepiece, the piece of glass at the opposite end of the scope.

A Ray of Light

Scientists wanted to know how the telescope's lens collected light from distant stars and what this light was made of. The study of light was felt to be very important, as the French scientist René Descartes noted in his essay "Discourse on the Method," published in June 1637. He wrote:

> The entire conduct of our lives depends on our senses, among which that of sight being the most universal . . . there is no doubt that inventions which serve to augment its power are the most useful which could exist. . . . And it is difficult to find any which increase it more than those marvelous glasses which, being in use only a short time, have discovered for us new stars in the sky and other new objects . . . in greater number than those which we had seen before: So that by carrying our vision much farther than the imagination of our ancestors, they seem to have opened to us the way to attain a much greater and more perfect knowledge of nature.[18]

The French scientist René Descartes believed that the telescope was the most useful invention in the world because it increased the power of sight.

Galileo's discoveries about the planets, moons, and stars started a revolution in scientific thought, but they left many questions unanswered. Some scientists were quick to begin studying the skies, looking for new information about celestial bodies. Others began to delve into the mystery of light. They wanted to know how the light from distant stars and the sun traveled to earth and what the light was made of. While most scientists were interested in looking for answers to these questions, some refused to accept any new discoveries. These scientists insisted that only Aristotle's ideas should be followed, especially in the area of light. In his lectures,

Aristotle classified sunlight and starlight as pure light or white light. Aristotle taught that color was a mixture of pure light and darkness. He believed that colors were created when light mixed with darkness or earthly matter and absorbed some of the matter. For example, a small mixture of darkness with white light created the color red, a larger percentage of darkness created the color blue.

Scientists who followed Galileo's ideas believed that darkness was not a substance, but merely the absence of light, and therefore could not be responsible for producing colors. These people believed that color was produced by some modification of light, but they were unable to explain how this happened. During the early 1600s, the French scientist Descartes developed a revolutionary theory that color was produced by the movement of tiny particles within a ray of light. Descartes believed that when these moving particles entered the eye, their motion was perceived as color. Descartes theorized that the human eye perceived fast-moving particles as the color red and slow particles as the color blue.

Endless Experimenting

Like all scholars of his day, Newton was well acquainted with Aristotle's theories. Newton also had the opportunity while at Cambridge to study Descartes's and Galileo's writings. The year before the plague struck, Newton bought his first prism and began experimenting with the refraction of light.

Intrigued with the nature of light, especially starlight, Newton spent countless nights working with his prism and searching the night skies until he fell ill from exhaustion. His illness, followed by the outbreak of the plague, interrupted his research until he left Cambridge for Woolsthorpe. There, Newton continued his experiments to understand the nature of light. He built grinding and polishing machines and began making his own lenses. He experimented first with spherical lenses and then began grinding new shapes to see how the shape of a lens affected the way it refracted light.

Newton did not limit his experiments to lenses and prisms. He was determined to understand how his eye was able to see light. During one of his first experiments, Newton spent days pressing on his eyeball

Intrigued by the nature of light, Newton experimented tirelessly with prisms and lenses, observing how they refract and distort light.

to see if the increased pressure would change the appearance of light. He stared at the sun and then plunged himself into a darkened room to see how the exposure to light and darkness would change his vision. Newton often endangered himself with his experiments. After staring at the sun in a mirror, Newton was forced to rest in a dark room for three days in order to recover. Newton wrote of his experiments in a letter to his friend John Locke:

> In a few hours I had brought my eyes to such a pass that I could look upon no bright object with either [eye,] but I saw the sun before me, so that I [could not] write nor read but to recover the use of my eyes shut my self up in my chamber [in the] dark for three days together and used all

means to divert my imagination from the Sun.[19]

Some of Newton's experiments were less dangerous and vastly more rewarding. While working with his prism, Newton made a basic discovery about the nature of light. Newton wrote to the secretary of the Royal Society, Henry Oldenburg, on February 6, 1672, telling of his experiments during this period. The Royal Society was a prestigious group of scientists dedicated to the motto *nullius in verba*, which translates to "take nobody's word for it; see for yourself." The organization unofficially began in 1645 when some of England's foremost scientists started meeting informally to share their ideas. One of the society's primary functions was to provide scientists with the means to test their experiments and ideas. The society also worked to bring the discoveries of its members to public attention. Gaining the society's interest was a mark of prestige for any scientist, and the society was very interested in Newton's work. Newton gave a detailed account of his experiments with light in his letter to Oldenburg:

> In the beginning of the Year 1666 . . . I procured . . . a Triangular glass-prisme, to try [to see] therewith the celebrated *Phaenomena of Colours*. . . . Having darkened my chamber, and made a small hole in my [curtains], to let in a convenient quantity of the Suns light, I placed my Prisme at its

In 1672 Newton wrote to Henry Oldenburg, the secretary of the Royal Society. The letter revealed Newton's important discovery about the composition of light.

entrance, that it might be thereby refracted to the opposite wall. It was at first a very pleasing [pastime] to view the vivid and intense colours produced thereby.[20]

Chasing Rainbows

In the experiment he described to Oldenburg, Newton allowed a beam of sunlight to shine through a small hole pierced in a heavy curtain. He positioned his prism so that the beam passed through it and formed a circular shape on the wall opposite the window. During this experiment he found something strange. The image on his wall was oblong, not circular like the hole through which the light had passed. By passing through the prism, the light was altered. At first Newton thought this change might have been caused by a flaw in his prism, and he tried a series of different pieces of glass. He also tried moving the prism outside the curtain so that the light struck the prism first and then passed through the curtain. But all these experiments created the same result—an oblong image on the wall. By continuing to experiment, Newton discovered that the white light consisted of a variety of different colored rays. When light went through a prism it was refracted, or bent, and separated into its various colors. This bending appeared to separate white light into its components because each of the colored rays of light had a slightly different refractiveness. This means each color of light bent a little differently when it passed through the prism, producing the array of colors on the wall. These experiments would later lead Newton to his the-

A page from a scientific work by J. T. Desaguliers illustrates Newton's prism experiment, in which sunlight is separated into its composite colors.

ories on the composition of light. But once again, Newton put his work aside without sharing it with anyone. The plague was ending and it was time for Newton to return to Cambridge.

During his two years of isolation in Woolsthorpe, the young scholar had made great discoveries in the history of science, but he was not ready to share them with the world. Newton was still relatively young and lacked the reputation that would bring ready acceptance of his ideas. Instead, Newton kept his discoveries to himself and returned to Cambridge to build his reputation as a scholar and a scientist.

3 Recognition

In March 1667 Newton left the quiet countryside and returned to the bustling halls of Cambridge. With the end of his years of quiet contemplation and discovery came the beginning of his rise to fame.

Once back at Cambridge, Newton quickly achieved success. Within six months he attained the status of minor fellow, or junior professor, and a few months

Upon his return to Cambridge, Newton quickly achieved success. Within months he attained the position of major fellow.

later became a major fellow, the equivalent of a senior professor. This transition marked the end of his student years and the beginning of his life as a professional scientist.

Although Newton easily passed his exams, the process of becoming a fellow of Cambridge was long and exhausting. Candidates for the position of major fellow spent three days answering questions from a group of senior professors and one day writing an in-depth theme on a topic chosen by their examiners. Newton passed all his examinations and on July 7, 1668, he received a master of arts degree from the university and became a major fellow. In this position, Newton was expected to tutor students and received a yearly stipend from the university for his work.

The Road to Fame

Only one year after graduation, on October 29, 1669, the university chose Newton as Lucasian Professor of Mathematics. This prestigious position was named after Henry Lucas, a member of Parliament, who donated money and land to Cambridge in 1663 to pay for the post. Lucas made his donation so that Cambridge

University could develop a quality mathematics program. At the time, the field of mathematics was gaining national attention. Many of the foremost scholars and politicians of the day had little, if any, training in mathematics. Samuel Pepys, for example, a well-educated man and a secretary of the British admiralty, knew so little arithmetic in 1665 that he had to hire a special tutor to teach him division. But as science progressed, so did people's interest in math. Lucas wanted to ensure that Cambridge would not be left behind in the scientific revolution, so he created a new professorship. The Lucasian chair quickly became a coveted position at Cambridge. In a period of only eight years, Newton was able to rise from the menial rank of *subsizar* to the position of Lucasian professor, one of the highest honors in the scientific community.

Mentor Isaac Barrow aided Newton's rapid rise. According to Newton biographer Stukeley, "The Doctor had a vast opinion of his pupil and would frequently say that he truly knew somewhat of mathematics, still he reckoned himself but a child in comparison of Newton."[21]

After reading Newton's first paper on mathematics, Barrow was convinced that Newton was the perfect person to succeed him. The paper that secured Newton's appointment was titled *De Analysis per Aequationes Infinitas* (On Analysis by Infinite Series). This paper, which contained the basic ideas Newton developed during his years at Woolsthorpe, would later be used to develop his theory of fluxions. The paper also ended Newton's years of obscurity and brought him national attention.

The events which led to Newton's rise to fame were set in motion in September 1668, when mathematician Nicholas Mercator published a paper titled *Logarithmotechnia*. Mercator's paper dealt with some of the basic ideas that Newton had discussed in *De Analysis*. In July 1669, John Collins, a member of the Royal Society, sent a copy of the book to Barrow. Barrow promptly wrote Collins about *De Analysis*, saying that the paper was written by a friend who had "an excellent genius" at math. Newton was still hesitant to share his ideas with the world, but finally, after much pressure from Barrow, Newton allowed his teacher to send the paper to Collins. Barrow, at his student's insistence, included a note reading: "I send you the papers of my friend I promised, which I presume will give you much satisfaction; I pray, having perused them so much as you think good, [return] them to me; according to his desire."[22] Collins was enthusiastic about the paper and promptly sent copies of it to the Royal Society and to various scientists and mathematicians.

The Lucasian Chair

Once Newton's work had sparked the interest of the Royal Society, Barrow had no trouble convincing the university to appoint him to the Lucasian chair. This appointment gave Newton ample money to live on and time to pursue his experiments. In his new post, Newton was required to lecture only once a week during one term a year and be available twice a week for student conferences. Neither the lectures nor the conferences demanded much of Newton's time, as mathematics was not a popular subject among Cambridge students. Lack of students was a chronic problem for both Barrow and

Newton. As Barrow remarked on the first anniversary of his appointment to the Lucasian professorship,

> I have sat on my Chair incessantly alone—and I am sure none of you will, as an eye-witness, challenge the accuracy of that statement even if I should be lying. . . . [I inhabit] this large and commodious domicile alone and undisturbed by a jostling and contentious crowd [of students].[23]

Like his predecessor, Newton lectured to empty rooms. As one of his biographers remarked, Newton, "for want of Hearers, read (to the) Walls."[24] The few students who did attend Newton's lectures found them hard to understand. Newton's first lecture series was on optics and consisted of

Teacher and mentor Isaac Barrow greatly admired Newton and helped him secure the position of Lucasian professor.

thirty-one speeches delivered without repetition between January 1670 and 1672. The lack of students hardly disturbed Newton, however, who enjoyed having the time to pursue his experiments in nature and optics.

Through the Eye of the Telescope

Newton's interest in optics led him to build a revolutionary telescope which produced a clearer image for its size than any in existence at the time. This instrument, called the Newtonian Reflecting Telescope, brought Newton instant fame. Like earlier telescopes, Newton's consisted of a tube with lenses fitted at both ends. But unlike previous instruments, Newton's scope reflected light instead of refracting it.

Although early refracting telescopes revealed new wonders to the world, they had a number of problems. Because they bent, or refracted, light to gather and focus it at a single point, the images produced by the objective lens were blurry and often marred by a halo of color. These problems were caused by the composition of light which Newton discovered at Woolsthrope. Since each color in a ray of light bent a little differently when it passed through a piece of glass, they each came to focus at a slightly different point inside the telescope. Instead of recombining into one clear image, the colors remained slightly separated and produced a fuzzy image.

After performing his studies on light, Newton concluded that once light was refracted by a lens, it could not produce a clear image. Instead of looking for a way to perfect existing telescopes, Newton

A Far-Seeing Device

Shortly after building his first telescope, Newton wrote to an unnamed friend about his vision for his new instrument. In a letter written in 1672 and excerpted in Louis Trenchard More's biography of Newton, Newton describes his new invention.

"I promised . . . to give you an account of my success in a small attempt I had then in hand. . . . The instrument that I made is but six inches in length [but] . . . it magnifies about forty times in diameter, which is more than any six feet tube can do, I believe, with distinctness. But, by reason of bad materials, and for want of good polish, it represents not things so distinct as a six feet tube will do; yet I think it will discover as much as any three or four feet tube; especially if the objects be luminous. I have seen with it Jupiter distinctly round and his satellites, and Venus horned. Thus, sir, I have given you a short account of this small instrument, which, though in itself contemptible, may yet be looked upon as an epitome of what may be done according to this way, for I doubt not but in time a six feet tube may be made after this method, which will perform as much as any sixty or hundred feet tube made after the common way; whereas I am persuaded, that were a tube made after the common way of purest glass, exquisitely polished, with the best figure that any geometrician . . . hath or can design . . . yet such a tube would scarce perform as much more as an ordinary good tube of the same length. And this, however it may seem a paradoxical assertion, yet it is the necessary consequence of some experiments, which I have made concerning the nature of light."

The success of the Newtonian Reflecting Telescope (pictured) inspired Newton to build a bigger and better model.

built an entirely new type of instrument. Newton replaced the telescope's lenses with mirrors. Since mirrors did not bend light, the images they produced were clear and bright. Newton replaced the lens at the end of the telescope with a curved mirror called the main mirror. Near the other end of the telescope tube, he placed a smaller mirror called the flat. In this type of telescope, the main mirror reflects light onto the flat. The flat is placed at an angle to reflect light into the eyepiece.

Newton wrote of his telescope to an unnamed friend in February 1689. "The instrument that I made is but six inches in length, [but] . . . it magnifies about forty times."[25]

The Royal Society Takes Notice

Word of Newton's invention reached the Royal Society. The group was intrigued by the telescope and asked its inventor to send one to the society. In response, Newton quickly built a second telescope and sent it for their inspection. The instrument roused much interest throughout the scientific body and various members built their own telescopes based on Newton's design.

While most members were excited by Newton's invention, one member, Robert Hooke, was envious of the attention the young English scholar was receiving. Hooke, who was to play a large role in Newton's life, was the curator of experiments for the society when Newton's telescope arrived. Hooke's job was to try the experiments suggested by society members and report his findings to the society. Hooke felt this to be one of the most important roles of the society, stating, "The truth is, the science of Nature has been already too long made only a work of the brain and the fancy: It is now high time that it should return to the plainness and soundness of observations on material and obvious things."[26] Robert Hooke was a man with great scientific abilities and an

A scientist performs an experiment for fellow members of the Royal Society. Society members were intrigued by Newton's telescope.

inquiring mind. If he had lived before Newton, he probably would have been remembered as one of the greatest scientists of his time. But he lived at the same time as Newton, and again and again Newton's brilliance outshone his own. Hooke's rivalry with Newton started with Newton's telescope.

As curator of experiments, Hooke was one of the first members to examine Newton's telescope. Not wishing the younger man to receive much praise, Hooke claimed that he had produced a similar telescope years earlier. In a memo to the society, member John Collins wrote that

> Mr. Hooke . . . affirmed . . . that in the year 1664 he made a little tube of about an inch long to put in his [telescope] which performs more than any telescope of fifty feet long, made after

the common manner; but the plague happening which caused his absence, and the fire [in London] whence redounded profitable employments about the city, he neglected to prosecute the same, being unwilling the glass grinders should know any thing of the secret.[27]

There is no evidence that the society, accustomed to Hooke's jealous nature, took his claims seriously. The group gave full credit for the reflecting telescope to Newton.

Unaware of Hooke's claims, Newton continued working on his scope and presented his third version to the Royal Society sometime during 1671. The society was so impressed with Newton's two telescopes that they voted to accept him as an official member of the society on January 11, 1672.

It's All Done with Mirrors

In the following letter, dated January 1672, and excerpted in Daniel J. Boorstin's The Discoverers, *Henry Oldenburg, secretary of the Royal Society, thanks Newton for sending one of his reflecting telescopes to the society.*

"You have been so generous, as to impart to the [scientists at the Royal Society] your Invention of the [reflecting] Telescopes. It having been considered and examined here by some of the most eminent in Optical Science and practice, and applauded by them, they think it necessary to use some means to secure this Invention from the Usurpation of foreigners; And therefore have taken care to represent by a [claim] that first Specimen, sent [here] by you, and to describe all the parts of the Instrument, together with its effect, compared with an ordinary, but much larger, Glasse . . . thereby to prevent the [theft of the idea] . . . it being too frequent, that new Invention and contrivances are snatched away from their true Authors by . . . bystanders."

Newton and his telescopes so impressed Royal Society members that they voted to accept him as an official member in 1672.

In a letter to Oldenburg written on January 6, 1672, Newton expressed his surprise:

> At the reading of your letter I was surprised to see so much care taken about [ensuring the] . . . invention [was credited] to me, of which I have hitherto had so little value. . . . Had not the [information about it] been desired, [I] might have let it still remain in private as it hath already done some years. . . . I am very sensible of the honour done me . . . in proposing me candidate [for the society], and which I hope will be further conferred upon me by my election into the society. And if so, I shall endeavour to testify my gratitude by communicating what my poor and solitary endeavours can effect towards the promoting [of] your philosophical designs.[28]

The Nature of Light

Newton was enthusiastic about membership in the society and promptly sent Oldenburg a lengthy letter on February 6, 1672. The paper outlined his discoveries on the composition of white light. Oldenburg received the letter on a morning when the Royal Society was scheduled to have a public meeting. The entire meeting was devoted to reading and discussing Newton's letter. In his letter, Newton outlined the experiments and theories he developed in his darkened room at Woolsthorpe.

Newton wrote that color did not come from light mixing with different sources, or from being changed by passing through a piece of glass. Instead, he asserted, color was a basic part of the light itself. As he wrote in his paper to the Royal Society,

Colours are not qualifications of light, derived from refractions, or reflections of natural bodies (as is generally believed,) but original . . . properties, which in divers rays are diverse. Some rays are disposed to exhibit a red colour, and no other; some a yellow, and no other; some a green, and no other; and so of the rest. Nor are there only rays proper and particular to the more eminent colours, but even to all their intermediate gradations.[29]

Through his experiments, Newton found that each color in a ray of light had its own degree of refractiveness. He found that the most refractive, or bendable, light rays were those with a deep violet color, and that red light rays were the least refractive. Newton also found that the color of a light ray could not be changed using external sources. After separating a colored ray of light by passing it through a prism, he tried shining the light through a piece of colored glass, but the light did not change color.

Unlike many of his later works, Newton's first treatise on light was clear, concise, and easy to understand. From his

When Newton tried to publish his discoveries about the composition of light, he encountered unexpected opposition. Many scientists refused to accept his theories because they contradicted traditional ideas about light and color.

notes he selected his most pertinent experiments and used these to support his theories. Most scientists published all their notes when publishing a paper, even those that had little bearing on the final theory. This practice made most scientific papers confusing and boring. In comparison, Newton's was exciting and lively.

The Royal Society applauded Newton's letter and voted to publish it as soon as it had been studied by the society. Members immediately gave it to Hooke's committee to analyze. Newton was pleased by the society's response, but his triumph was short-lived. Newton expected that his experiments would be challenged, but he was not prepared for the reaction his paper produced. As the paper circulated, Newton found that many esteemed scientists of his day refused to accept his theories because they did not conform to the traditional ideas of light and color. Instead of trying to recreate Newton's experiments, they denounced his work.

Controversy

One of the first scientists to criticize Newton's work was Hooke. During the next meeting of the Royal Society on February 15, 1672, Hooke reported:

I have perused the discourse of Mr. Newton about colours and refractions, and I was not a little pleased with the niceness and curiosity of his observations . . . yet as to his hypothesis of solving the phenomena of colours. . . . I confess, I cannot see yet any undeniable argument to convince me of the certainty thereof. For all the experiments and observations I have hitherto made, nay, and even those very experiments, which he allegeth, do seem to me to prove, that *white* [light] is nothing but a pulse or motion . . . and that colour is nothing but the disturbance of that light . . . that *whiteness* and *blackness* are nothing but the plenty or scarcity of the undisturbed rays of light.[30]

Newton responded to Hooke's criticism by saying "[I] am glad that so acute an objecter [as Hooke] hath said nothing that can [disprove] any party of [the paper]. . . . I . . . doubt not but that upon severer examinations it will be found as . . . truth . . . as I have asserted it."[31] In his reply, Newton barely refrained from calling Hooke a liar by inferring that Hooke had not had time to perform any experiments to disprove his work.

The controversy over Newton's paper continued for two years, growing more heated as time passed. One of Newton's most vehement opponents was Professor Linus of Liège. Linus's paper titled "Philosophical Transactions" was published by the Royal Society on October 6, 1674. In the paper, Linus accused Newton of gross carelessness and intentionally misrepresenting the results of his experiments. Oldenburg was troubled by Linus's accusations and urged Newton to refute the paper publicly. By this time, Newton was tired of the debate and wanted to retreat from the public limelight. Newton declined to enter the debate in a letter written to Oldenburg on December 5, 1674. In the letter, Newton stated, "I have long since determined to concern myself no further about the promotion of philosophy. And for the same reason I must desire to be excused from engaging to exhibit . . . philosophic discourses."[32]

A Public Quarrel

Controversy and public arguments over his work plagued Newton throughout most of his career. In a private letter to Henry Oldenburg, secretary of the Royal Society, Newton directs Oldenburg to supply information about his experiments to some of the more vocal critics in the hopes of silencing them. The following letter is excerpted from John William Navin Sullivan's Isaac Newton.

"I am sorry you put yourself to the trouble of transcribing Fr. Linus's conjecture, since (besides that it needs no answer) I have long since determined to concern myself no further about the promotion of philosophy. And for the same reason I must desire to be excused from engaging to exhibit . . . philosophic discourses, but yet cannot but acknowledge the honour done me by your council, to think of me for one amongst that list of illustrious persons, who are willing to perform it, and therefore desire to have my thanks returned to them for the motion. . . . If you think fit you may, to prevent Fr. Linus's slurring himself in print with his wide conjecture, direct him to the scheme in my second answer to P. Pardies [another critic], and signify . . . that the experiment, as it is represented, was tried in clear days, and the prism placed close to the hole in the window, so that the light had no room to diverge, and the coloured image made not parallel, (as in his conjecture,) but transverses to the axis of the prism."

Newton did not like public disputes and decided to withdraw from the controversy. In January 1676, Hooke also appeared to have had his fill of the controversy and wrote to Newton suggesting they discuss their scientific differences in private. In a letter dated January 20, 1676, Hooke wrote, "I do [not] approve of contention or feuding and proving in print and shall be very unwilling drawn to such kind of war."[33]

Newton responded to Hooke on February 5 stating that he was "exceedingly well pleased and satisfied with your generous freedom and think you have done what becomes a true Philosophical spirit. There is which I desire to avoyde in matters of Philosophy more than contention, nor any kind of contention more than one in print: and therefore I gladly embrace your proposal of a private correspondence."[34]

Satisfied that the controversy was finished and determined never to share his ideas publicly again, Newton returned to his experiments.

4 Years of Discovery and Challenge

Determined never again to enter into another public dispute of his work, Newton focused again on his experiments. But Newton seemed destined to be involved in one scientific brawl after another. Despite his resolve, Newton was drawn back into the arena only six months after vowing to leave public life forever.

The Fluxion Dispute

Newton's second fight started at the same time as the first, and was with a German mathematician named Gottfried Wilhelm Leibniz. Leibniz had developed a new type of mathematics which he called calculus. This form of math was very similar to Newton's method of fluxions. The main difference between the two types of math was the notation system each used, but the basic idea behind each system was the same. Newton's friends, fearing that Leibniz would get credit for ideas that Newton had developed first, urged Newton to publish a paper on his fluxion method. It was important for the creator of an idea or invention to publish it so that he could establish ownership. Public acclaim, and perhaps monetary rewards, were often heaped upon the scientist who made an

important discovery. Scientists who waited too long to announce their discoveries risked seeing someone else develop their ideas, and the first to publish was usually the one who received credit for the discovery. And Newton waited too long. While Newton was the first to discover the math

Because Newton waited too long to publish his fluxion method, German mathematician Gottfried Wilhelm Leibniz received credit for discovering calculus—the math we use to measure motion.

we use to measure motion, the name it goes by and the notation system we use today is the one developed by Leibniz.

At first Newton refused to listen to his friends. Finally, on June 13, 1676, he sent Oldenburg a letter outlining his discoveries shown in *De Analysis*, the paper which had won Newton the Lucasian chair at Cambridge. While Newton alluded to his method of fluxions, he did not explain the theory in his letter. Newton explained to Oldenburg that "it still lacks being a universal method without some further method of extending infinite series—How this may be done, there is not now time to explain."[35] Oldenburg read the letter to the Royal Society on June 15 and forwarded the document to Leibniz.

Sharing Ideas

Leibniz wrote immediately to Newton requesting more information on his formula. "Newton's discoveries are worthy of his genius, which is abundantly made [clear] by his optical experiments and by his [reflecting telescope]," Leibniz wrote to Oldenburg on August 27, 1676.[36] Newton replied with a nineteen-page letter discussing math in general, but giving no further explanation of his fluxions. Newton included in the letter a jumble of letters that formed an incomprehensible sentence: "I cannot proceed with the explanation of [the fluxions] now, I have preferred to conceal it thus: 6accdae13eff7i3l9n404qrr4s8t12vx."[37] The sentence contained an anagram which represented letters in a Latin phrase that translated to "given any equation involving any number of fluent quantities, to find the fluxions, and vice versa." Even

Although Newton desired credit for being the first to develop the fluxion method, he remained reluctant to publish his work.

translated, the phrase has little meaning. If Leibniz could have unscrambled the puzzle he still would have known nothing about Newton's method. Using anagrams to protect scientific discoveries was a common practice in the seventeenth century. Using the anagram was a form of insurance for Newton. Newton believed that if anyone developed a form of the fluxion method, he could translate the anagram and prove that he had developed the method first. Being cautious, Newton did not put valuable information about the method in the anagram in case Leibniz was able to unscramble it. The same day he replied to Leibniz, Newton sent a note to Oldenburg saying, "I hope this will so far satisfy Mr. Leibnitz, that it will not be necessary for me to write any more about this subject; for having other things in my head, it proved an unwelcome interruption to me to be at this time put upon considering these things."[38]

Pressure to Publish

Newton's friends continued to pressure him to publish his entire method of fluxions. But Newton adamantly refused. In a letter to John Collins on November 8, 1676, Newton wrote:

> You . . . desire that I would publish my method, and I look upon your advice as an act of . . . friendship . . . [but] I could wish I could retract what has been done [the publishing of the theory of light], but by that I have

learned . . . to let what I write lie . . . till I am out of the way.[39]

Newton remained silent on the subject until June 1684 when he received a letter from David Gregory, a Scottish mathematician who recently had been appointed to a mathematical chair at Edinburgh, a position similar to Newton's. Gregory was anxious to publish the mathematical papers of his uncle, James Gregory, but first he wanted Newton's opinion. Upon reading the papers, Newton realized that the pages held ideas which could be developed into a type of mathematics which could be used in the field of motion. If Gregory continued his uncle's work, his math could develop into a system very similar to Newton's method of fluxions. At the same time, Newton was hearing more about Leibniz's brilliant new mathematics. The time had come, Newton was convinced, to publish his fluxion method.

Newton's paper, titled "Specimens of a Universal System of Mathematics,"

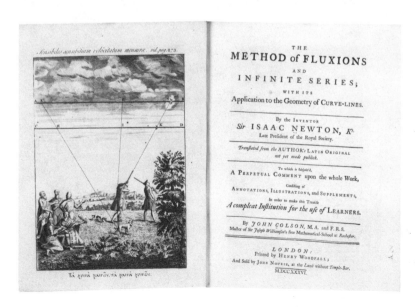

Despite pressure by colleagues, Newton adamantly refused to publish his works. Consequently, his treatise on the fluxion method was not published until nine years after his death.

contained six chapters which outlined his method. He also included all of his correspondence with Leibniz as well as a translation of the anagram he had sent to the German scientist. But just as the manuscript was nearing completion, Newton abandoned it. Once again, he was hesitant to enter a public brawl, so he postponed publication of his work.

Newton's Friends Come to His Defense

While Newton delved into other scientific areas, Leibniz published his own paper. Word reached Newton of Leibniz's publication in the spring of 1685, but he did not respond at the time. Though Newton was unwilling to enter the battle, his friends were not. On December 18, 1691, Newton follower Nicolas Fatio de Duillier wrote, "It seems to me from everything that I have been able to see so far . . . that Mr. Newton is beyond question the first Author of the differential calculus and that he knew it well or better than Mr. Leibniz yet knows it."[40] Two months later Fatio sent another letter implying that Leibniz had borrowed ideas from Newton. The controversy continued to heat up, as Leibniz followers suggested that perhaps Newton had stolen the German scientist's ideas. In 1699 Fatio wrote a scathing defense of Newton's work:

> I now recognize, based on the factual evidence, that Newton is the first inventor of this calculus, and the earliest by many years; whether Leibniz, the second inventor, may have borrowed anything from him, I should rather leave to the judgement of those who

have seen the letters of Newton and his other manuscripts. Neither the silence of the more modest Newton, nor the unremitting exertions of Leibniz to claim on every occasion the invention of the calculus for himself, will deceive anyone who examines these records as I have.[41]

Around the same time, mathematician John Wallis, another Newton follower, printed the third volume of his *Mathematical Works*. This included more detailed accounts of the early correspondence between Leibniz and Newton than had been published previously. While they did not prove that Leibniz took his ideas from Newton's fluxions, the letters lent some proof to Fatio's claims that Leibniz had gained mathematical knowledge from

Mathematician John Wallis was one of many followers who agreed that Newton was the first to develop calculus.

Very few people, including the best educated scientists of the day, could fully understand Newton's Principia. *Newton made his new book intentionally difficult. In a letter to an unnamed friend, Newton explained his book. The following is taken from John William Navin Sullivan's* Isaac Newton.

"I had, indeed, composed the third Book, in a popular method, that it might be read by many; but afterwards, considering that such as had not sufficiently entered into the principles could not easily discern the strength of the consequences, nor lay aside the prejudices to which they had been many years accustomed, therefore, to prevent the disputes which might be raised upon such accounts, I chose to reduce the substance of this Book into the form of [mathematical] Propositions which should be read by those only who had first made themselves masters of the principles established in the preceding Books; not that I would advise anyone to the previous study of every Proposition of those Books; for they abound with such as might cost too much time, even to readers of good mathematical learning."

Newton. Leibniz replied with an anonymous attack in 1704, comparing Newton with Honoré Fabri, a French plagiarist. Newton, though still unwilling to come to the forefront of the battle, was outraged. Instead of answering Leibniz himself, he began to rally his followers against the German scientist. One, John Keill, a Scottish mathematician who was Newton's pupil at Cambridge, wrote that "Fluxions, which Mr. Newton, without any doubt, first invented; . . . the same arithmetic, under a different name . . . was afterwards published by Mr. Leibniz."[42]

The fight might have become more bitter and proceeded more swiftly if Newton had not been involved in another project. Newton was too caught up in his research to devote a great amount of time and energy to defeating Leibniz. While the calculus controversy raged around him, Newton was completing his greatest scientific achievement—the *Principia.*

The Puzzle of Universal Gravitation

Newton may never have developed his greatest work if not for his rivalry with Hooke. Hooke's insults and public boasting had spurred Newton into motion. The actions leading to the *Principia* began in January 1684, in a small, English bar where three scientists—Christopher Wren, Edmond Halley, and Robert Hooke—were discussing the construction of the universe. Newton's friend Halley had raised a question: How did gravity affect the planets and

Christopher Wren (pictured) challenged Edmond Halley and Robert Hooke to answer the question: What keeps the planets in orbit around the sun?

it public. However I remember, that Sir Christopher was little satisfied that he could do it; and though Mr. Hooke then promised to shew it [to] him, I do not find, that . . . he has been so good as his word.[43]

Unable to solve the problem himself or to obtain an answer from Hooke, Halley journeyed to Cambridge that August to see Newton. What would the path of a planet look like if gravity was acting on the body? Halley asked his friend. Newton was able to answer Halley's question instantly. The path of a planet would be an ellipse. Newton had solved the question years before, sitting beneath an apple tree at Woolsthorpe. When Halley asked for a copy of his proofs, Newton could not find the work he had performed almost twenty years before. Newton promised to recreate

Unable to solve the problem himself, Edmond Halley (pictured) turned to Newton, who provided an immediate answer.

what kept them in orbit around the sun? The scientists also wondered what the path of a planet's orbit around the sun would look like, if gravity was holding the planets in orbit. Halley wrote of the meeting:

> Mr. Hooke affirmed, that . . . all the laws of the celestial motions were to be demonstrated, and that he himself had done it. I declared the ill success of my own attempts; and Sir Christopher, to encourage the enquiry, said he would give Mr. Hooke, or me, two months' time, to bring him a convincing demonstration thereof; . . . Mr. Hooke then said that he had it, but he would conceal it for some time, that others trying and failing might know how to value it, when he should make

While pondering planetary motion, Newton developed the theory of universal gravitation.

his mathematical papers and send them to Halley. By November, Newton had completed the problem and sent it to his friend. Halley was impressed by Newton's work and sent a copy of Newton's paper to the Royal Society in December 1684.

Halley's question inspired Newton's interest in gravity once again. Also, Hooke's arrogant claims that no one other than himself would be able to solve the problem of gravity spurred Newton to investigate the topic further. Newton began working on a set of theorems to give a general explanation of planetary motion. But he developed much more than that. Newton's experiments resulted in a theory that explained how gravity acted as the glue holding the entire universe together.

A Storm of Creation

As he developed his theory, Newton worked like a man possessed by demons.

He neglected his health, his appearance, and his friends. He walked about the university with his hair unbrushed, his coat unbuttoned, and his garters undone so that his socks sagged around his ankles. He forgot to eat meals, sometimes ignoring his breakfast tray until dinner time. According to Humphrey Newton, one of his assistants at Cambridge during this time:

> He very rarely went to bed till two or three of the clock, sometimes not until five or six, lying about four or five hours, . . . [spending weeks in] his laboratory, . . . going out either night or day . . . till he had finished his . . . experiments, in the performance of which he was the most accurate, strict, exact . . . . His pains, his diligence at these . . . times made me think he aimed at something beyond the reach of human art and industry. . . .[44]

According to his assistant, Newton was so engrossed in his thoughts he paid little attention to the world around him. Humphrey Newton wrote:

The Absentminded Professor

Newton was a true absentminded professor. Humphrey Newton (no relation to Isaac) served as his assistant from 1685 to 1690. Later, Humphrey wrote of his years with the professor. The following is excerpted from H.D. Anthony's Sir Isaac Newton.

"His carriage was then very meek, sedate, and humble, never seemingly angry, of profound thought, his countenance mild, pleasant, and comely. I cannot say I ever saw him laugh but once. . . . He always kept close to his studies, very rarely went a visiting, and had . . . few visitors. . . . I never knew him to take any recreation or pastime either in riding out to take the air, walking, bowling or any other exercise whatever, thinking all hours lost that [were] not spen[t] in his studies, to which he kept so close that he seldom left his chambers. . . . So intent, so serious upon his studies, that he ate very sparingly, nay, ofttimes he has forgot to eat at all, so that, going into his chamber, I have found his [meals] untouched, of which, when I have reminded him, he would reply—"Have I?" and then making to the table, would eat a bit or two standing, for I cannot say I ever saw him sit at table by himself. He very rarely went to bed till two or three of the clock, sometimes not until five or six, lying about four or five hours. . . . I cannot say I ever saw him drink either wine, ale or beer, excepting at meals, and then but very sparingly. He very rarely went to dine in the hall, except on some public days, and then if he not been [re]minded, would go very carelessly, with shoes down at heels, stockings untied . . . and his head scarcely combed. . . . I believe he grudged the short time he spent in eating and sleeping. . . . In a morning he seemed to be as much refreshed with his few hours sleep as though he had taken a whole night's rest."

Some . . . times when he [planned] to dine in the hall, [he] . . . would turn to the left . . . and go out into the street [instead of to the dining hall], when making a stop when he found his mistake, would hastily turn back, and then sometimes instead of going into the hall, [he would forget he was going to eat and] would return to his chamber again. . . . [45]

Newton completed work on the first of the three books which make up the *Principia* in only seventeen months. The book was dedicated to the Royal Society and presented to its members on April 28, 1686. Many of the members were away from London at the time, and those present voted to give Newton's work to Halley for examination. Halley was directed to report on the book at the society's next meeting. The records of the May 19, 1686, meeting do not mention the spirited debate caused by Newton's work. The official records simply state that the society voted to have "Mr. Newton's [book] . . . printed forthwith."[46] But in a letter to Newton following the meeting, Halley warns his friend that Hooke claimed Newton's discoveries were actually his.

The *Principia*

The *Principia* rekindled the feud between Newton and Hooke. After reading the *Principia*, Halley wrote to Newton on May 22, 1686, that

> Mr. Hooke has some pretensions [about the book]. . . . He says you had the notion from him, though he owns the demonstration . . . to be wholly your own. . . . Mr. Hooke seems to expect you should make some mention of him in the preface. . . . I must beg your pardon, that 'tis I that send you this ungrateful account; but I thought it my duty to let you know, . . . being in myself fully satisfied, that nothing but the greatest candour imaginable is to be expected from a person, who has of all men the least need to borrow reputation.[47]

Newton was furious with Hooke's charges. He responded to Halley's letter by writing that Hooke

has done nothing, and yet written in such a way, as if he knew . . . [but excused himself from the work of proving his ideas] by reason of his other business, whereas he should rather have excused himself by reason of his inability. For 'tis plain, by his words, he knew not how to go about it.[48]

Newton also refused to give Hooke credit for any of his ideas. As Newton wrote to Halley:

> Now is not this very fine? Mathematicians that find out, settle and do all the business must content themselves with being nothing but dry calculators and drudges and another that does nothing but pretend and grasp at all things must carry away all the invention[s] of [others]. . . . And why should I record a man for an Invention who founds his claim upon an error . . . [and then] gives me trouble? He imagines he obliged me by telling me his Theory, but I thought my self disobliged by being . . . [told by Hooke of] a Theory which everybody knew and I had a truer notion of [than] himself. Should a man who thinks himself knowing and loves to [show his knowledge by] correcting and instructing others, come to you when you are busy, and . . . press discourse upon you . . . and then [when you develop a better theory he will] boast that he taught you all . . . and oblige you to acknowledge it and cry out injury and injustice if you do not, I believe you would think him a man of a strange and unsociable temper.[49]

Newton's anger at Hooke's claims almost kept him from publishing the last

PHILOSOPHIÆ

NATURALIS

PRINCIPIA

MATHEMATICA.

Autore JS. NEWTON, Trin. Coll. Cantab. Soc. Matheseos Professore Lucasiano, & Societatis Regalis Sodali.

IMPRIMATUR.

S. PEPYS, Reg. Soc. PRÆSES.

Julii 5. 1686.

LONDINI,

Jussu Societatis Regiæ ac Typis Josephi Streater. Prostat apud plures Bibliopolas. Anno MDCLXXXVII.

Newton's Principia, *published in 1686, was an immediate success.*

two books of the *Principia.* On June 20, Newton wrote to Halley that

> I designed the whole to consist of three books . . . [but now I] design to suppress [the third book]. Philosophy is such an impertinently litigious Lady, that a man had as good be engaged in lawsuits, as have to do with her. I found it so formerly, and now I am no sooner come near her again, but she gives me warning.[50]

Only the knowledge that he would be harming his friend by not publishing the books kept Newton from suppressing them. Halley, acting for the Royal Society, was in charge of printing the books. And,

since the society had so little money, the relatively poor Halley agreed to pay for the printing himself. In turn, Halley would receive a percentage of the profits raised from the books. If Newton did not finish the entire work and the books did not sell, his friend would be bankrupt. Writing to his friend about his change of heart at the end of June, Newton said, "I am very sensible of the great kindness of the gentlemen of your society to me, far beyond what I could ever expect or deserve."[51] In his letter, Newton told the society he resolved to finish his books in memory of the society's past kindness toward him. Newton wrote that he would not hold the society responsible for the actions of one member. No matter how angry Hooke made him, Newton promised to finish his book. Newton delivered the second book on March 1, 1687, and the third on April 4. After countless publishing delays, the book was published during the summer of 1687 and sold for 10 shillings.

Initial Reaction

The *Principia* was an immediate success and the first printing of the book, to the surprise of even Halley, sold out instantly. The scientific revolution was under way, and both scholars and lay people were interested in science. Many of the scientists who bought the *Principia* became enthusiastic supporters of Newton's theories. Scottish mathematician David Gregory wrote to Newton on September 2, 1687, saying, "Having seen and read your book I think my self obliged to give you my most hearty thanks for having been at pains to teach the world that which I never expected any man should have knowne."[52] Teachers at the Universities of St. Andrew and Edinburgh were so impressed with the *Principia* that they began teaching Newton's theories in class. That is, those of his theories that they could understand.

The *Principia* was a very difficult work, even for the most well educated scholars of Newton's time. Philosopher Richard Bentley, after struggling to understand the manuscript, asked Newton to suggest a course of study that would prepare him to understand the complex math in the book. The list of required reading was so long that Bentley decided to give up his study of the *Principia*. "The reading of the preliminary list alone would consume a greater part of my life," he said.[53]

Newton did not understand why the public thought his work difficult. "The principles of my theory are within the intellectual grasp even of those who are unacquainted with the higher mathematics. For the book deals merely with the simple laws of matter," Newton argued. Theories in the *Principia* would give anyone the power to unravel the mysteries of nature, he asserted.

> Just give me the mass, the position and the motion of a system of heavenly bodies at any given time, and I will calculate their future positions and motions by a set of rigid and unerring mathematical calculations. . . . I will calculate the tides and the motions of the waters and the earth. For the earth attracts the moon and the moon attracts the earth . . . and the force of each in turn tends to keep both in a state of perpetual resistance. Attraction and reaction—reaction and attraction. . . . The great masses of the planets and the stars remain suspend-

Philosopher Richard Bentley was not the only well-educated scholar who found Newton's Principia *too difficult to understand.*

ed in space and retain their orbits only through this mysterious law of universal gravitation.[54]

An Attractive Theory

In its simplest form, Newton's theory stated that every particle of matter attracts every other particle with a force equal to the product of the two bodies' mass. It also said that the force of the attraction between the two bodies decreases with greater distance between the two bodies. Newton's theory destroyed forever the idea that the sun, moon, and stars had a special, mystical place in the universe. According to the *Principia*, all matter—from the highest stars above to the earth on

Newton Loses His Temper

Newton's rivalry with Hooke resurfaced as Newton prepared to publish the Principia. *Hooke wanted Newton to acknowledge him in a preface to the book. In a letter to his friend Edmond Halley written June 20, 1686, Newton denounces Hooke's claims. This excerpt is taken from Louis Trenchard More's biography of Newton.*

"Mr. Hooke has erred in the invention he pretends to, and his error is the cause of all the stir he makes. . . . Why should I record a man for an invention, who founds his claim upon an error therein, and on that score gives me trouble? He imagines he [gave the information to] me by telling me his theory . . . [that] I had a truer notion of than himself. Should a man who thinks himself knowing, and loves to show it in correcting and instructing others, come to you, when you are busy, and not withstanding your excuses press discourse upon you, and through his own mistakes correct you . . . and then . . . boast that he taught you all he spake, and oblige you to acknowledge it, and cry out injury and injustice if you do not; I believe you would think him a man of strange and unsociable temper. Mr. Hooke's letters in several respects abounded too much with that humor, . . . this is the third time that he has given me trouble of this kind."

which we walk—obeyed the same principle. Newton also solved the mystery of what caused the tides to rise and fall, a puzzle that scholars had tried to solve for thousands of years. Newton wrote that "the flux and reflux of the sea arise from the actions of the sun and moon."[55] The work also contained three laws of motion which are still the basis for studying motion. These laws said that a body at rest stays at rest, and a body in motion stays in motion, unless acted on by some outside force; a body in motion will change its direction of motion in proportion to the force exerted upon it; and to every action there is always an opposite and equal reaction. These ideas, which were so simple to Newton, were far beyond most scholars of his day.

Some, even though they did not understand it, protested Newton's work because it seemed to violate religious teaching.

Newton's idea that the planets and tides moved in accordance with mechanical laws, not simply by the will of God, caused some scientists to quickly challenge Newton's theory. His critics called the ideas explained in the *Principia* "deranged poetical fancy" and declared that Newton would "not have twenty followers in his lifetime"[56]

Weary from his months of labor and confused by the public's lack of understanding of his work, Newton retreated from public life. As the *Principia* became an international sensation, its author found himself on the brink of a mental and physical collapse.

Chapter

5 The Price of Genius

Newton was exhausted after completing the *Principia*. His friends and colleagues were alarmed at his irrational behavior, and rumors that Newton had suffered a complete mental collapse spread quickly. Newton had often behaved oddly in the past, shunning companions and continuing his research throughout the night, especially when he was intent on solving a difficult problem. Many of Newton's earlier discoveries had been made during periods of intense concentration and seclusion, but not to the extent that he had imposed on himself while writing the *Principia*. Newton had been known to miss a meal or two, and perhaps a night's sleep, but during the eighteen months of intense work on the *Principia*, he went for several days at a time without food or sleep.

Newton's Greatest Loss

The physical strain on Newton's body was enough to weaken his health severely, but a series of events shortly before and after his work on the *Principia* no doubt contributed to his breakdown. One of the most devastating blows was the death of his mother, Hannah. Even though Newton

was miles away at Cambridge, he remained very close to his mother and was considered her favorite child. They wrote each other frequently, and he traveled

Following completion of the Principia, *Newton exhibited irrational and often eccentric behavior. Friends and colleagues speculated that he had suffered a complete mental breakdown.*

often to Woolsthorpe to see her. Conduitt states that

> he made frequent journeys from Cambridge to visit [Hannah] and even at that time when he was in the warmest pursuit of those enchanting discoveries which made him forget his food and his rest and seemed to transport his imagination above all sublunary things, broke loose to pay his duty to her.[57]

When Hannah fell deathly ill with a fever that had nearly killed Newton's half-

Newton greatly admired John Locke's strong moral convictions and great intellect. Their close friendship lasted until Locke's death in 1704.

brother, Benjamin Smith, Newton sat with her and tried to nurse her back to health. Newton left Cambridge and took the longest absence of his academic career to care for her and "[sat] up whole nights with her . . . gave her all her [medicine] himself, dressed all her blisters with his own hands, and made use of that manual dexterity for which he was so remarkable."[58] All his efforts were in vain, however. After nearly a year of illness, Hannah died in the same house where she had given birth to Isaac many years before. She was buried June 4, 1679, leaving Newton completely alone. Newton spent nearly six months at Woolsthorpe settling her estate before returning to his scholarly life at Cambridge. He retreated into his solitary studies and mourned his loss in private. Though he was deeply involved in writing the *Principia* by 1684, Hannah's death still weighed heavily on Newton. His friends described him as more aloof and melancholy than ever before.

Newton Reaches Out

In addition to his mother's death, four close friends of Newton died or became quite ill around this time. Isaac Barrow, Newton's mentor and close friend at Cambridge, died suddenly in 1677. Henry Oldenburg died in 1678. John Collins died in 1683 after several years of debilitating illness, and Henry More died in 1687. By the time the *Principia* was published in 1687, many of Newton's most valued and trusted friends were gone. The weight of these losses wore him down and contributed to his anguished mental state. For the first time in many years, Newton began to seek out new acquaintances and became receptive to gestures of friendship. He met many new people as men of learning sought him out to discuss the ideas he had put forth in the *Principia*. Two of these were John Locke and Nicolas Fatio de Duillier.

In Locke, Newton found a kindred spirit, a man of great intellect and strong personal beliefs. As Gale Christianson writes in *In the Presence of the Creator*, "In Locke Newton also found one of the very few who merited his implicit trust, a man who had chosen exile over moral and political compromise, a man who shared a substantial part of his larger vision of things—past, present, and future."[59] Locke also had an underlying compassion for the shy and aloof scholar and treated him with great respect and understanding. Their friendship lasted until Locke's death in 1704 and was a reassuring presence in Newton's life.

Newton's other friend, Fatio, proved more influential, but not in a positive way. Fatio was an ardent admirer of Newton and often referred to Newton as "the greatest mathematician ever to have lived and the most worthy gentleman [I have] ever met."[60] Newton was flattered by Fatio's devotion and was impressed with his talents in astronomy and mathematics.

Newton saw Fatio as a younger version of himself, and the two quickly became close friends. The loss of his longtime and cherished friends like Barrow and Collins induced Newton to overcome his natural reserve and invite Fatio into his inner circle much sooner than he ordinarily would have. They shared many common interests beyond mathematics, including astronomy, medicine, and alchemy. (Alchemy was a medieval chemical science. Its chief aim was the conversion of base metals, like lead, into gold.) Newton felt that Fatio could be a great mathematician and encouraged him as he had aided and encouraged many promising young men in the past.

The End of a Friendship

Evidence of Newton's fatherly affection appeared when, upon learning that Fatio was ill, Newton wrote to urge his friend to leave London for Cambridge. He said that "I feare [the] London air conduces to your indisposition and therefore wish you would remove hither so soon as [the] weather will give you leave to take a journey. For I believe this air will agree with you better." Later, Newton even offered help with lodging and money, writing that

> the chamber next me is disposed of; but that which I was contriving was, that since your want of health would not give you leave to undertake your design for a subsistence at London, to make you such an allowance as might make your subsistence here easy to you.[61]

Newton soon came to depend on Fatio's mathematical abilities and selected Fatio to edit and correct the second edition of the *Principia*, a task Newton had never allowed anyone else to do. But by the time Newton was ready to begin his work on the revised edition, the close friendship had dissolved. No one knows what caused Newton to turn away from Fatio, but no one doubts that losing his closest friend of the time added stress to Newton's life and contributed to his breakdown.

A Scholar No More

The final factor in Newton's collapse may be attributed to his growing dissatisfaction with his scholarly life. Newton had never been at ease with his teaching duties at Cambridge and now enjoyed them even less. He felt that his contributions to science, which brought glory to England, should be rewarded with a royal appointment. In Newton's lifetime, an appointment from the king was considered a sinecure. A sinecure is a position that pays a good salary but requires little or no work. The royal appointments were prestigious and paid well, but usually had little to do with the actual work of running the country. Newton felt he deserved such a position. Newton's friends felt it was a disgrace that the scientist did not have a royal appointment. A mutual friend, John Millington, wrote to Samuel Pepys that it was "a sign of how much it [learning] is looked after, when such a person as Mr. Newton lies so neglected by those in power."[62] Though Newton had the scientific community's respect, he was still unable to obtain the royal recognition that he felt was his due.

Newton's disappointment was even more pronounced after his success with the *Principia*. The publication of the *Principia* had brought Newton immense public recognition, though few people actually read the work and fewer could understand what they had read. Newton felt that his increasing international reputation should have ensured him a royal appointment, but none was offered. Finally, Newton began to ask his friends who had ties to the royal court to help him obtain an appointment. But even his most influential friends were unable to provide him with the kind of position he sought. As the appointment continued to be withheld,

Most people remember Newton for his contributions as a scholar, as he is depicted in this statue in Westminster Abbey. His dissatisfaction with scholarly life, however, prompted him to seek a royal appointment.

Following the publication of the Principia, *Newton was physically and mentally exhausted. In the following letter, written to Samuel Pepys in September 1693 and excerpted in John William Navin Sullivan's* Isaac Newton, *the scientist describes his condition.*

"Some time after Mr. Millington had delivered your message, he pressed me to see you the next time I went to London. I was averse; but upon his pressing consented, before I considered what I did, for I am extremely troubled at the embroilment [I] am in, and have neither ate nor slept well this twelve-month, nor have my former consistency of mind. I never designed to get anything by your interest, nor by King James's favour, but am now sensible that I must withdraw from your acquaintance, and see neither you nor the rest of my friends any more, if I may but leave them quietly. I beg your pardon for saying I would see you again, and rest your most humble and most obedient servant."

Newton became suspicious that his friends were not supporting him. He grew bitter and depressed and began to withdraw from his friends and society.

The Price of Genius

In September 1693, Newton wrote several disturbing letters to his friends John Locke and Samuel Pepys. To Pepys he stated "I am extremely troubled . . . and have neither ate nor slept well this twelve-month, nor have my former consistency of mind. . . . I must withdraw from your acquaintance, and see neither you nor the rest of my friends any more."[63] Newton wrote to Locke, apologizing for "having hard thoughts of you [Locke]." He went on to say that he had been "of opinion that you endeavored to embroil me with women and by other means"[64] and begged Locke's forgiveness.

Both Pepys and Locke were confused and upset by the rambling letters, and neither recognized the incidents to which Newton was referring. Pepys was sure some terrible misunderstanding had occurred and quickly called upon John Millington to visit Newton and discover what was wrong. Pepys wrote that he feared Newton had been inflicted with "a discomposure in head, or mind, or both" and urged Millington to speak to Newton immediately, saying, "I own too great an esteem for Mr. Newton . . . to be able to let any doubt [of my actions] concerning him lie a moment uncleared."[65] Newton was only able to apologize and say that he was very ashamed. He added that he had written Pepys after "a distemper that much seized his head, and that kept him awake for about five nights together."[66]

Samuel Pepys expressed great concern about the mental state of his friend Newton.

Newton's friend Locke fared no better when he responded to Newton's rambling, apologetic letter in mid-September. Locke had written back immediately, saying:

[G]ive me leave to assure you that I am more ready to forgive you than you can be to desire it and I do it soe freely and fully [that] i wish for noe thing more than the opportunities to convince you [that] I truly love and esteem you and [that] i have still the same good-will for you as if noe thing of this had happened.[67]

Locke was greatly concerned about his friend's health and their friendship and urged Newton to meet with him to work out any difficulties. Newton could not remember any of the accusations he had hurled at Locke. He could only explain his own strange behavior in a short letter

A Letter of Apology

While Newton was recovering from writing the Principia, *he withdrew from society and became paranoid even of his friends. In a letter to John Locke in September 1693, Newton wrote of his feelings. The following is taken from John William Navin Sullivan's* Isaac Newton.

"Being of opinion that you endeavoured to embroil me with women and by other means, I was so much affected with it, as that when one told me you were sickly and would not live, I answered, 'twere better if you were dead. I desire you to forgive me this uncharitableness. For I am now satisfied that what you have done is just, and I beg your pardon for my having hard thoughts of you for it, and for representing that you struck at the root of morality, in a principle you laid down in your book of ideas, and designed to pursue in another book, and that I took you for a Hobbist. I beg your pardon also for saying or thinking that there was a design to sell me an office, or to embroil me. I am your most humble and unfortunate servant, Is. Newton."

Rumors spread that Newton's mental breakdown was the result of his grief over papers lost in a fire. According to some, the fire erupted when Newton accidentally upset a candle in his laboratory.

that repeated what he had told Millington earlier. He ended his letter very uncharacteristically by saying, "I remember I wrote to you but what I said of your book I remember not. If you please to send me a transcript of that passage, I will give you an account of it if I can."[68] Newton had never been so lavish with apologies or so willing to admit his mistakes or his forgetfulness. This worried his friends even more.

Noted scientist and astronomer Christian Huygens recorded the following details in his journal and in a letter to Leibniz:

> On the 29th May, 1694, a Scotchman of the name of Colin, informed me, that Isaac Newton, the celebrated mathematician, eighteen months previously, had become deranged in his mind, either from too great application to his studies, or from excessive grief at having lost, by fire, his chemical laboratory and some papers.[69]

Rumors spread at the time that Newton had accidently upset a candle in his labo-ratory and the resulting fire burned some of his papers. No one is sure what, if any, papers were actually destroyed. News of Newton's mental illness continued to circulate. But by June, Leibniz was able to assure Huygens that he was "happy that I received information of the cure of Mr. Newton, at the same time that I first heard of his illness, which, without doubt, must have been most alarming. It is to men like Newton and yourself, Sir, that I desire health and a long life."[70]

By May 1694 Newton seemed to have recovered completely, but his recovery was as mysterious as his breakdown. Newton never spoke of his illness, aside from his apologetic letters, but he never again experienced such an intense creative period as he did during the creation of the *Principia*. He concentrated his scientific efforts on refining his theories on light and color, calculus, and performing alchemical experiments. But his main occupation became obtaining a respected and honorable appointment from the king. Finally his efforts were rewarded. At a time when England was undergoing a great monetary crisis, Newton was appointed warden of the Royal Mint.

Warden of the Mint

Prior to Newton's appointment, most people who received a sinecure did very little work. This practice changed forever when Newton took his new position at the mint. The previous wardens had just sat back and collected their pay, barely supervising the mint workers. As a result, theft and inefficiency plagued the mint. Prior to Newton's appointment, about fifteen thousand pounds of silver were made into coins each week. The coins produced were irregularly shaped and sized. This was partly due to the workers' indifference and partly to the mint's production methods. In 1662 a mechanical press had been introduced to make a more uniform coin, but it had proved so awkward and difficult to use that most of England's coins were still made by hand. The coins were cut from sheets of silver with large metal shears. They were trimmed to roughly the correct size and shape, then finished with a round stamp and a hammer. The edges were plain and smooth, and each coin was slightly different in size and weight from any other coin. Seldom did two coins contain the same amount of silver.

Since no one expected the coins to be uniform, it was easy for counterfeiters to copy or alter existing coins by "clipping." Clipping was done by snipping or filing small amounts of silver from the coin's edges. The silver could then be melted down and used to produce counterfeit coins. The clipped coins recirculated at their full face value, even though they contained less silver and were worth less. Counterfeiting and clipping were so common that it was almost impossible to find a genuine coin in its original condition.

The counterfeiting, along with the irregular coins put out by the mint, caused many disturbances in England's economy.

An illustration depicts the minting of coins at the Royal Mint in London. Prior to Newton's appointment as warden of the Royal Mint, the coins produced were irregularly shaped and sized.

Workers were paid with coins that were supposed to be worth a certain amount in silver, but in fact were worth much less. When the workers tried to buy goods or pay their debts, the merchants refused to accept the coins at face value, insisting that the coins be weighed to determine their true worth in silver. When weighed, the workers' coins were worth much less than the amount they represented. The situation had worsened to the point that fights between employers and workers, merchants and customers occurred nearly every day, and small riots burst out on paydays.

The Great Recoinage

In 1695, King William ordered the Great Recoinage. He ordered that all the old coins be recalled, melted down, and made into new coins. The king also specified that the new coins be produced in a way that made them difficult to counterfeit or alter. Charles Montague, chancellor of the exchequer, was in charge of this huge project. Montague knew he would need a completely honest and meticulous person to supervise the necessary changes at the mint. Montague knew that Newton had accused him of deserting him and of neglecting their friendship. He saw this as a great opportunity to help Newton obtain the prestigious position he had sought for so long. Montague, sensitive to Newton's feelings of abandonment, wrote: "I am very glad that I can give you good proof of my friendship and the esteem the King has of your merits. . . . The King has promised me to make [you] Warden of the Mint."[71]

Newton took his new position seriously. He zealously prosecuted thieves within the mint and counterfeiters on the streets. Newton made his viewpoint on punishment for counterfeiting plain in a letter to Lord Townshend, a minister to the king, about one particular case:

> I know nothing of Edmund Metcalf convicted . . . of counterfeiting the coin; but since he is very evidently convicted, I am humbly of opinion that it's better to let him suffer, than to venture his going on to counterfeit the coin again, for these people seldom leave off. And it's difficult to detect them.[72]

Newton also appointed new deputies to oversee the outlying branches. He soon began issuing official rebukes to mint officials.

To combat counterfeiting and improve England's economy, King William ordered the Great Recoinage in 1695.

In an attempt to repair their damaged friendship, Charles Montague, chancellor of the exchequer, offered Newton the position of warden of the mint.

Early on, Newton sought to sever the ties between the mint and the military. The mint and its branches were located on large tracts of land, and on part of this land were barracks housing area soldiers. While guarding the mint was only one of the soldiers' many official functions, the king felt that quartering the soldiers near the mint helped safeguard it. Although the soldiers' proximity did increase security at the mint, the soldiers also caused many problems. The soldiers were constantly fighting with one another or with civilians who worked at the mint. Newton was quick to step in whenever a problem arose with the military. On hearing that an officer at the Chester branch had challenged another officer to a duel, Newton sent them a stern message, saying:

We are much concerned to hear of your continued quarrels . . . we believe both sides much in the wrong and resolve to come and hear of it ourselves. . . . Till we come let there be no further quarreling . . . for the Mint will not allow of the drawing of swords and assaulting of any, nor ought such language we hear has been, be used any more amongst you.[73]

The disagreements between mint workers and the military were an old problem that Newton decided to resolve immediately. The soldiers and civilian mint workers were often involved in heated disputes. Soldiers harassed the workers, sometimes arrested them for little or no reason, and searched their houses randomly. Newton became a champion of the mint workers, writing to Montague at the treasury that

the [soldiers] begin to be rather a grievance th[a]n security to us. . . . Why should every [soldier] be impowered under any feigned pretense to shoot his enemy or any other man that complains, if such bloody discipline may safely be avoyded? Or why should the people who live in the mint be so terrified as to leave their habitations in it to the neglect of the Kings service and insecurity of the treasure?[74]

He strongly appealed to Montague to recognize the mint as an institution outside the military's control, arguing that the banks and merchants would lose faith in the stability of the mint if the soldiers' "invasions" were not stopped. Newton bluntly stated, "We were placed in a Garrison that the Exchange and Treasury of the Nation might not be invaded by our Guards but guarded in our custody from all manner of invasion."[75]

Taking Up the Reins

At the same time Newton sought to establish the mint's independence from the military, he also requested a broad increase in his own authority. He pointed out that the duties of warden had gradually passed to the minor officials of the mint, and that "those Ministers act as they please for turning the Mint to their several advantages. Nor do I see any remedy more proper and more easy th[a]n by restoring the ancient constitution."[76] When Newton took office, clerks who reported to the warden had taken over all the day-to-day work at the mint. They were responsible for everything, from overseeing the workers to deciding where and how supplies were bought. The warden was viewed as a figurehead with no control over the mint's operation. Newton wanted to regain control of the operations and run it as he thought necessary. Montague was happy to give Newton all the power he requested, as the Great Recoinage had begun and England was beginning to feel the effects.

When Newton arrived at the mint in April 1696, ten new furnaces for melting the recalled coins had already been built. Thousands of pounds of coins had been collected to be made into new coins. Newton increased the number of workers and shifts in order to place a great quantity of new coins back into circulation. It was vital to England's economy that the mint produce the new coins quickly. Montague had declared that the old coins would no longer be accepted after May 4, 1696. If enough new coins were not available, panic and riots could occur. With his efficient and firm administration, Newton was able

---

Warden of the Mint

Newton finally won a position as warden of the Royal Mint. Friend Charles Montague wrote to Newton of the position in 1696. The following is taken from Louis Trenchard More's Isaac Newton, A Biography.

"I am very glad that at last I can give you a good proof of my friendship, and the esteem the king has of your merits. Mr. Overton, the Warden of the Mint, is made one of the Commissioners of the Customs, and the king has promised me to make Mr. Newton, chief officer in the Mint. 'Tis worth five or six hundred pounds per annum, and has not too much business to require more attendance than you may spare. I desire you will come up as soon as you can, and I will take care of your warrant in the meantime. . . . Let me see you as soon as you come to town, that I may carry you to kiss the king's hand. I believe you may have a lodging near me. I am, Sir, your most obedient servant, Chas. Montague."

The Tower of London contained the mint during Newton's time. Newton's zeal and skill as warden helped make the Great Recoinage a success.

to increase production to £120,000 a week. By August, the money situation had stabilized, and the mint, under Newton's watchful eye, was running smoothly.

By 1699, the Great Recoinage was completed. It was a success due to men like Montague, Halley, Locke, and Newton who had helped form the new monetary plans. During his years as warden, Newton set aside his mathematical and philosophical studies to devote all his energy and skills to his appointed position. A letter to fellow astronomer John Flamsteed in 1699 indicated Newton's new priorities. As Newton wrote, "I do not love to be printed on every occasion . . . or to be thought by our own people to be trifling my time about them [mathematical problems] when I should be about the King's business."[77]

A Scientific Challenge

Although Newton refrained from most scientific debates during this time, he still could not refuse a challenge. In 1696, scientist Johann Bernoulli published a challenge to all mathematicians in the world: to find the path, other than a straight vertical line, along which a body would fall in the shortest amount of time. Bernoulli thought the path would turn out to be a curve, even though a straight line was the shortest distance between two points. Newton received a copy of the challenge from Bernoulli and was able to solve the problem the same night. Newton agreed with Bernoulli. The fastest path for a ball to travel would be a curve known as cycloid,

In 1696, scientist Johann Bernoulli (below) published the following challenge to all scientists: to find the path, other than a straight vertical line, along which a body would fall in the shortest amount of time. Newton's solution, the cycloid (above), was derived in one night and published anonymously. Bernoulli, however, knew immediately who its author was.

or a shape that resembles a half-circle. By rolling balls along two tracks, one a straight line inclined at a forty-five-degree angle and the other in the shape of a half-circle, Newton found the ball in the circular track traveled faster. The steepness of the curve in the initial part of the cycloid made the ball accelerate faster than the ball traveling the same distance along the straight line. Newton published his solution to the problem anonymously. But when Bernoulli read Newton's paper, he knew immediately who the author was. "The lion," said Bernoulli, "is known by his claw."[78] Only Newton, Bernoulli asserted, could have solved the problem so quickly and so eloquently. After Bernoulli's challenge, Newton refrained from other scientific inquiries and devoted his energy to the mint.

Along with the everyday problems of running the mint, Newton also was plagued with repeated attempts by powerful people to bribe him. Newton's friend Reverend Derham wrote of one such incident:

He [Newton] told me that an agent of one had made him an offer of above 6000 pounds, which [he] refused on account of its being a bribe, the agent said he saw no dishonesty in the acceptance of the offer, and that Sir Isaac understood not his own interest. To which Sir Isaac replied, that he knew well enough what was his duty, and that no bribes should corrupt him. The agent then told him, that he came from a great Duchess. . . . To which Sir Isaac roughly answered, "I desire you to tell the lady, that if she was here herself, and had made me this offer, I would have desired her to go out of my house; and so I desire you, or you shall be turned out."[79]

Newton's ability to carry out Montague's recoinage plan, along with his efficient and honest administration of the mint's daily business, did not go unnoticed. On December 25, 1699, Newton was promoted to the highest position at the mint, master of the mint. It was unusual for a warden ever to move up to the master position. Only once before, during the reign of Elizabeth I, had a warden risen to the position of master of the mint. But Newton was a model of integrity at a time when most appointed officials were known for their greed and dishonesty. Newton officially resigned his position at Cambridge and served the king as master of the mint for thirty years. He became the ideal to which other public servants were compared.

Chapter

6 The Final Years

The final years of Newton's life were rich in terms of social status and public recognition. Through his work as a scientist and as master of the mint, Newton's fame continued to spread and brought him to the attention of kings and princes around the world. World leaders had heard of Newton's discoveries and reputation as one of the leading scientists of the world. These men were anxious to learn from Newton, or for the scientists attached to their courts to learn from him and bring this knowledge back to their home countries. One of Newton's most unexpected visitors was Peter the Great, ruler of Russia.

Accolades from Royalty

On February 5, 1698, Newton received a cryptic note from his kinsman Sir John Newton. It said, "The Czar intends to be here tomorrow . . . and I thought my self obliged to [tell] You he likewise expects to see You here. I have taken all possible care to have things in readiness and have not time to add more."[80] Peter the Great, czar of Russia, had journeyed to England to learn from the scientist who had written the *Principia*. The meeting between Newton and the czar was private, and little is

known about what transpired between them. But the czar was sufficiently impressed by Newton that upon returning to Russia, he implemented reforms in the Russian coinage system based on Newton's example.

The Russian czar was only the first of Newton's many royal admirers. When

Newton's fame brought him many prestigious admirers and visitors, including Peter the Great, czar of Russia.

The royal court directed Newton to oversee the design of medallions in honor of Queen Anne's coronation. His design, which portrayed Anne as a Greek goddess, delighted the queen.

Queen Anne ascended to the throne on April 23, 1702, she directed Newton to personally oversee the design of a medallion in honor of her coronation. Newton's design, gold and silver medallions stamped with a picture of Anne portrayed as a Greek goddess, was a great success with the

In 1705 Queen Anne conferred knighthood upon Newton, one of the highest honors given by the royal family.

queen and her guests. Newton made eighteen hundred of the medals for distribution to dignitaries during the ceremony.

Newton continued to be a favorite of the royal court. Members of the royal family read Newton's works, and his papers and public squabbles became a favorite topic at court. Newton was even called upon by Princess Caroline to help select a course of study for her children. In April 1705, Queen Anne bestowed upon Newton one of the highest honors the crown could convey. The queen journeyed to Cambridge and knighted three men: John Ellis, vice-chancellor of the university; James Montague, university counsel; and Isaac Newton. As described by Sir David Brewster in his papers, "The Queen held a court at Trinity Lodge, where she rendered this day memorable, by conferring knighthood upon the most illustrious of her subjects, Sir Isaac Newton."[81] With Newton receiving so much attention from the royal family, the study of science became a fashionable pursuit. Foreign ambassadors to England and nobles vied for membership in the Royal Society as if it were an exclusive club. Newton's own longtime membership in this organization eventually brought him the second-greatest honor of his life.

Reviving the Royal Society

Newton's rise in the Royal Society was made possible by the death of Newton's chief rival, Robert Hooke, on March 3, 1703, at the age of sixty-eight. On November 30 of that year, the society assembled to elect new officers. Following some political maneuvering by his supporters, Newton was chosen president with twenty-six votes. Once elected, Newton held the position for almost twenty-five years and during that time dramatically changed the society.

When Newton assumed the presidential post, the Royal Society was on the verge of collapse. Almost bankrupt, the society's membership had declined by almost a thousand members in a period of five years, and the remaining members had become fascinated with trivial curiosities instead of science. Newton's reform plan, named a "Scheme for Establishing the Royal Society," called for a return to the study of science through experimentation and for the creation of a staff of four paid employees. The staff members were required to attend all meetings and to present experiments and lectures in the areas of chemistry, optics, math, astronomy, zoology, and chemistry. This change ensured that scientific topics would be the society's main concern.

Newton's plan also was designed to make the organization solvent again. Beginning in 1706, every candidate for admission to the society had to pay an admission fee and sign a pledge for his weekly dues before being admitted. In addition, no members behind in their dues could serve on the council. A clerk was appointed to call upon those who were behind in their dues and try to collect the outstanding amount. Those who failed to bring their accounts current risked having their names stricken from the society's membership roster.

Taking Charge

While putting his plan into effect, Newton also worked to gain absolute control over the society. Newton and his followers used every opportunity to remove Newton's rivals from positions of power. One example occurred in May 1706, when the outspoken Dr. John Woodward, a science professor at Gresham, was removed from the governing board of the society for having publicly insulted another member during a meeting. Although this offense was relatively minor, Newton used any excuse to oust members who challenged his authority.

Newton passed a series of orders designed to make the society a more serious organization and to increase the power of its president. Among others, these orders stated that only the president was allowed to sit at the head of the table and no member was allowed to talk during a meeting without first addressing the president. Newton's early biographer, Stukeley, described meetings of the Royal Society under Newton's reign:

> Whilst he presided in the Royal Society, he executed that office with . . . grace and dignity—conscious of what was due to so noble an Institution. . . . There were no whispering, talking nor loud laughters. . . . Every thing was transacted with great attention and solemnity and decency; . . . [the meetings were held] without any levity.[82]

An engraving of a Royal Society meeting, with Newton presiding. As president of the society, Newton instituted a number of reforms designed to make the society a more serious organization.

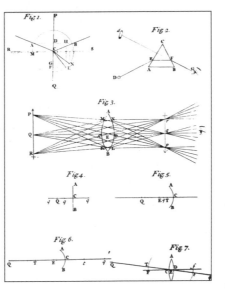

OPTICKS:

OR, A

TREATISE

OF THE

REFLEXIONS, REFRACTIONS,

INFLEXIONS and COLOURS

OF

LIGHT.

ALSO

Two **TREATISES**

OF THE

SPECIES and MAGNITUDE

OF

Curvilinear Figures.

LONDON,

Printed for SAM. SMITH, and BENJ. WALFORD,
Printers to the Royal Society, at the *Prince's Arms* in
St. *Paul's* Church-yard. MDCCIV.

The title page and a plate from Newton's Optics, *which included the research on light and telescopes he had completed years before, but had delayed publishing for fear of public dispute.*

Those who did not follow the rules were removed from the meeting.

Optics

Hooke's death and Newton's powerful position as president of the Royal Society gave Newton the security he needed to turn his attention back to science. Newton felt so secure that he decided to publish his complete work on the field of optics. Unlike his earlier *Principia*, Newton's *Optics* was published with little fanfare. The first mention of the book is a note in the Royal Society records on February 16, 1704: "The President [Newton] presented his book of Optics to the Society. Mr. Halley . . . desired to . . . [read] it and give an abstract of it to the Society. The Society gave the President their thanks for the Book and for his being pleased to Publish it."[83] In the foreword to the book, Newton said *Optics* was the result of research he had completed years earlier but delayed publishing. "To avoid being engaged in Disputes about these matters, I have hitherto delayed the printing, and should still have delayed it, had not . . . Friends prevailed upon me."[84]

Optics contained detailed accounts of the phenomena of reflection and refraction, the breakdown of white light as it passed through a prism, how images were formed by lenses, and the construction of the reflecting telescope. *Optics* was much easier to read and understand than the *Principia*. Unlike Newton's earlier work, *Optics* contained many experiments and few complex mathematical formulas. *Optics* was very successful and scientists used it as the focal point for research in the fields of chemistry, electricity, and magnetism.

Newton also used the publication of *Optics* to make another public stab at his longtime adversary, Leibniz. Newton included two sections in the book which explained some of his theory of fluxions. In the introduction to *Optics*, he explained the reason for including the fluxions by writing:

In a letter written to [Mr.] Leibniz in the year 1676 . . . I mentioned a method by which I had found some general theorems. . . . And some years ago I lent out a manuscript containing such theorems; and having since met with some things copied out of it, I have on this occasion made it public.[85]

Newton felt that Leibniz had stolen his ideas, and he wanted the world to know.

A Stellar Controversy

While the younger Newton had shied away from controversy, the elder Newton was no longer afraid of a good fight. During these years, Newton became autocratic and demanded obedience from his followers. Newton had little patience with those who failed his expectations. One of those who felt Newton's wrath was Royal Astronomer John Flamsteed, Newton's onetime friend.

Charles II had given Flamsteed the post of king's astronomer on June 2, 1675. Flamsteed established the Royal Greenwich Observatory; his mission was to study the night sky and develop an accurate catalog of the stars he observed.

Newton shared Flamsteed's interest in astronomy and at first, as members of the Royal Society, they were friends. Flamsteed even shared some of the data he had gathered at the observatory with Newton, who used the information in the *Principia*. But Flamsteed, like many scientists of the time, was wary of others stealing his discoveries. He felt that Newton had not given him enough credit in the *Principia* for his contributions. In return, Flamsteed angered Newton by publicly refuting some of Newton's theories about a comet that flamed through the sky in 1680.

Professional Fear and More Feuds

Newton and astronomer John Flamsteed joined in a bitter battle over Flamsteed's star charts. Flamsteed made note of the argument in his diary in 1717. The following is excerpted in Frank E. Manuel's A Portrait of Isaac Newton.

"[Newton's] design was . . . *to make me come under him* . . . force me to comply with his humours, and flatter him . . . as [his followers] did. . . . He thought to work me to his ends by putting me to extraordinary [tasks]. . . . *Those that have begun to do ill things, never blush to do worse and worse to secure themselves.* Sly [Newton] had still more to do, and was ready at coining new excuses and pretenses to cover his disingenuous and malicious practices. I had none but very honest and honorable designs in my mind: I met his cunning forecasts with sincere and honest answers, and thereby frustrated not a few of his malicious designs."

Relations between the two men were further strained in 1694, when Newton began pressing Flamsteed to share all his records. Newton was impatient to use Flamsteed's data to finish his own work about the movement of the moon. When Flamsteed resisted, Newton became demanding and began a series of political maneuvers to force the younger scientist to publish his work. Resentment and harsh words continued to flow in correspondence between the two men. In his diaries, Flamsteed called Newton's letters unkind and arrogant. Suffering from childhood illnesses which caused lifelong handicaps, Flamsteed was never in good health and he claimed that Newton's pressure was causing him blinding headaches. In response, Newton advised him to "bind his head strait with a garter till the crown of his head was nummed," and to continue his work.[86]

Newton and his onetime friend, astronomer John Flamsteed, became engaged in a bitter feud when Flamsteed refused to share his research with the scientific community. Newton used his power and influence to force Flamsteed to publish his work.

"In a Rage"

The tension continued to escalate as Newton tried to wrestle Flamsteed's star charts from him. The astronomer refused to yield; he did not want to publish anything until the charts were finished, a task that could continue for years. Finally, in 1704, Newton used his court influence to have the queen herself intercede by appointing Newton and a group of his followers as overseers of the Royal Observatory. This group had the power to force Flamsteed to release his findings. Flamsteed was outraged. In his diary, Flamsteed outlined a meeting he had with the committee. "All he [Newton] said was in a rage: he called me many hard names; *puppy* was the most

innocent of them. I told him only that I had all imaginable deference and respect for Her Majesty's order . . . but that it was a dishonor . . . to use me so."[87] But finally Newton won, and Flamsteed delivered his star charts in 1707. Even though Newton won the dispute, he never forgave Flamsteed for defying him.

Although Newton's scientific life during this period was filled with controversy, he managed to avoid any religious conflicts. Queen Anne explicitly stated that she would support only those who strictly followed the teachings of the Church of England. Even though Newton never openly admitted it, his writings indicate that he was a Puritan, and the beliefs of the Puritans were often contrary to the teachings of the Church of England. Because his personal beliefs did not conform to the church's views, Newton was careful to keep his beliefs private. Some of

William Whiston, Newton's successor to the Lucasian professorship, was banned from the university for his open defiance of the Church of England.

Newton's followers were not so skilled, and were tried for heresy, or crimes against the church.

One of those who came in conflict with the church was Newton's handpicked successor to the Lucasian professorship, William Whiston. Whiston published a series of his own sermons that challenged some of the traditional beliefs of the Church of England. In 1708, Whiston was ordered to retract his sermons, but he refused. Because of his open defiance of the church, in October 1710 Whiston was called before the leaders of the college, stripped of his professorship, and banned from the university. In 1711, Whiston published a manuscript titled *Historical Preface*

to Primitive Christianity Revived which mirrored many of the ideas Newton wrote about in his private papers. Historians believe that Whiston learned of the Puritan doctrines from his mentor Newton, but Newton would not support Whiston's religious rebellion. Instead he shunned his former follower.

Newton was so displeased with the way Whiston handled himself that when the Royal Society considered making Whiston a member in May 1716, Newton had his name removed from the list.

The Death of a Genius

Newton remained a powerful and autocratic leader of the mint and the Royal Society until 1724, when ill health overtook him. During that year, Newton's successors began to take over more and more of his duties at the mint. Often he was confined to bed for weeks at a time with gout and kidney problems, but he retained his position as president of the Royal Society. In January 1725, Newton developed a violent cough and inflammation of the lungs. His recovery took weeks, and afterwards his friends convinced him to move to a village outside the city where the air was cleaner. The move from London seemed to help the elderly scientist, and for a time his health improved. But on March 2, 1727, Newton presided over his last meeting as president of the Royal Society. The rigors of the trip to London from his village home took their toll on Newton. Upon returning home, Newton fell ill and never recovered. During his last few days, Newton remained alert and reflected on his life. While others were awed by his discov-

Prior to his death Newton remarked that his achievements were insignificant when compared to all that remained to be learned—a humble remark for a man who had achieved almost superhuman fame for his important discoveries.

eries, Newton saw his achievements as almost insignificant when compared to what remained to be learned. As he told one of his visitors shortly before his death:

> I do not know what I may appear to the world; but to myself I seem to have been only like a boy playing on the sea-shore and diverting myself in now and then finding a smoother pebble or a prettier shell than ordinary, whilst the great ocean of Truth lay all undiscovered before me.[88]

But Newton was forced to leave the rest of the ocean for his followers to explore. In the early hours of March 20, 1727, Newton died.

7 A Lasting Influence

During his life, Newton developed a theory that explained the way the universe functioned and tied the earth, sun, and planets together with one theory that united the cosmos. According to historian James Burke in his book *The Day the Universe Changed,*

With his theory of universal gravitation, the far-seeing Newton forever changed our view of the universe.

Newton's cosmology provided people with a universe that was comfortable and reliable within which to work and think. In his description of planets moving according to the same immutable laws which applied on earth, Newton showed that the natural state of society was a reasonable, stable, unrevolutionary one, in which . . . [there were] laws that governed men just as surely as they governed the stars. Newton had, after all, shown that change was produced by the application of lawful force which moved planets in orbit.[89]

For developing this new and rational view of the universe, Newton became known as more than just a scientist or researcher—he was worshipped as a national hero. The honors bestowed upon Newton at his death show the profound admiration the scientist commanded.

The Death of a Hero

Before Newton, the death of a scientist brought little public attention. Even the death in 1642 of Galileo Galilei, the Italian scientist who is often called the father of modern science, received little attention outside the scientific community. In contrast, Newton's funeral was a state affair. Newton's mourners included not only scientists, but also politicians and English royalty. After attending Newton's funeral, the French writer Voltaire commented that Newton was honored "like a king who had done well by his subjects."[90] The scientist was buried in Westminster Abbey, the traditional burial place of kings and queens that was denied to many members of the English nobility. Dukes and earls carried Newton's body in an elaborate casket to his final resting place. Final proof of Newton's acclaim can be found on his tomb. Its inscription reads:

> Sir Isaac Newton . . . Who, by a vigor of mind almost supernatural, first demonstrated the motions . . . of the planets . . . and the tides of the ocean. He diligently investigated the [refractability] of the rays of light and properties of the colours to which they give rise. . . . Let mortals rejoice that there has existed such and so great an ornament of the human race.[91]

A statue also was placed in the chapel of Trinity College at Cambridge in his honor. The inscription reads, "Newton, Who surpassed all men of genius."

Public Tribute

Newton also was honored by some of the outstanding poets of his time, including Henry Brooke and Alexander Pope. Brooke saw Newton as the "eternal founder" of all scientific thought who understood the workings of nature which were

The memorial marker on Newton's grave at Westminster Abbey, where he was buried alongside kings and queens.

beyond most people's comprehension. Brooke wrote:

> For deep, indeed, the Eternal founder lies,
> And high above his work the Maker flies;
> Yet infinite that work, beyond our soar.[92]

Pope wrote of him:

> Nature, and Nature's Laws lay hid in Night,
> God said Let Newton be! and All was Light.[93]

Newton was revered not only by the rich

and powerful, but also by common people. One French admirer went so far as to suggest that the British revise their calendar to start counting time from Christmas Day 1642, Newton's birthdate, in honor of the scientist.

Newton's work still rules the field of motion and Newton's terminology is still used to describe and predict the motion of objects. His theories on motion and mechanics are used to guide the paths of spacecraft, to predict the orbits of earth satellites, to design navigation and radar systems, to explore problems of space travel, and to test theories about ocean currents and the dynamics of the atmosphere. The reflecting telescope, which brought Newton much fame, is still vital to the field of astronomy. So significant were his achievements that historians break science into two periods, the years before Newton and those after. As historian Sir Herman Bondi said:

> There comes a . . . stage when it is so difficult to imagine what the world was like before a particular contribution that one can hardly get the contribution into perspective. The landscape has been so totally changed, the ways of thinking have been so deeply affected, that it is very hard to get hold of what it was like before. The landscape

---

Newton's View of the World

The French writer Voltaire attended Newton's funeral and was deeply touched by what he saw. In 1732, Voltaire wrote of his experiences in his work Letters Concerning the English Nation, *published in England in 1732. It is excerpted here from Jean-Pierre Maury's book* Newton, The Father of Modern Astronomy.

"A Frenchman arriving in London finds things very different, in natural sciences as in everything else. He has left the world full, he finds it empty. In Paris they see the universe as composed of vortices of subtle matter, in London they see nothing of the kind. For us it is the pressure of the moon that causes the tides of the sea; for the English it is the sea that gravitates toward the moon, so that when you think that the moon gives us a high tide, these gentlemen think it should have a low one. . . . Furthermore, you will note that the sun, which in France doesn't come into the picture at all, here plays its fair share. . . . The very essence of things has [been] totally changed [by Newton]. . . . He lived honored by his compatriots and was buried like a king who had done well by his subjects. . . . His great good fortune was not only to be born in a free country but at a time when, scholastic extravagances being banished, reason alone was cultivated and society could only be his pupil and not his enemy."

of physical science was so completely altered by Newton that it is very hard for us to realize how total of a change in outlook he produced.[94]

Influencing Future Generations

During his life, Newton changed the way the world viewed science. Through his work, science became part of daily life. Sailors and merchants used his studies to improve navigation at sea and to expand trade, and astronomers used his telescopes to expand our knowledge of the universe. Newton's works became such an integral part of society that a book, written especially for women and titled *Newtonism for the Ladies*, was published to explain his principles. Newton's ideas changed the way we look at the universe and were the result of his brilliant work and the dedication of his followers. Newton also influenced science through the lives of those he touched. During his last year of life, Newton devoted much time to fostering and shaping the careers of young scientists.

Among those Newton assisted was Scottish mathematician James Stirling, who was later known as a leading advocate of Newton's ideas. When Newton first learned of Stirling, the Scottish scientist had been forced to flee his homeland after becoming embroiled in politics. After reading some of the young scholar's papers, Newton was so impressed he decided to help Stirling. Newton sent him money and arranged to have the young man's works published in England. Newton's influence was so great that he was even able to have Stirling pardoned so that he could

Newton's likeness is forever preserved in a statue at Trinity College, Cambridge. Its inscription reads, "Newton, Who surpassed all men of genius."

return to his home country. Stirling, in turn, became a devout Newtonian. He once wrote to Newton, "As your generosity is infinitely above my merit, so I reckon myself ever bound to serve you to the utmost; and, indeed, a present from a person of such worth is more valued by me than ten times the value from another."[95] Stirling, through his experiments, writing, and years of teaching helped continue the spread of Newton's ideas.

Another Scottish mathematician, Colin Maclaurin, also received help from Newton. And like Stirling, Maclaurin devoted much of his life to building on the scientific foundations established by Newton. Maclaurin was a gifted mathematician and by the age of nineteen was appointed professor of mathematics at Marischal College in Aberdeen, Scotland. Maclaurin met Newton at the Royal Society and often said that Newton's friendship was the "greatest honour and happiness" of his life. Newton was impressed by the young professor and took an active interest in his career. When MacLaurin confided to Newton that he was a candidate for a prestigious position at the University of Edinburgh but was facing stiff competition, Newton resolved to help. In a letter to the provost of Edinburgh, Newton wrote, "I think he [Maclaurin] deserves it [the position] very well. And, to satisfy you that I do not flatter him, . . . I am ready . . . to contribute twenty pounds per [year] towards a provision for him."[96] Based on Newton's influence, Maclaurin was chosen for the position. In turn, Maclaurin was one of Newton's most vocal supporters. Maclaurin was the first to teach Newton's theories of fluxions and mechanics.

Color and Light

The experiments of English scientist John Dalton, born in 1766, expanded on Newton's work on color and light. Dalton developed a theory to explain the phenomena of color blindness. Many of Dalton's techniques were similar to those of Newton, and he was often compared to his countryman. In later life, Dalton even began to resemble Newton. When someone remarked on the uncanny resemblance, Dalton replied that it was "no miracle at all . . . [because] it was the selfsame [power of] mind that molded the features . . . of both."[97] The French naturalist Compte Georges-Louis Leclerc de Buffon used Newton's theories to expand the age of the earth. In 1749, Buffon used Newton's calculations to set the age of the world at 74,832 years, more than 24,000 years older than was previously thought.

While the work of many of Newton's followers was impressive, perhaps the most famous admirer of Newton to become a well-known scientist was Albert Einstein, whose ideas would replace many of Newton's almost two hundred years after his death. Einstein was an avid fan of Newton's—he had read all the English scientist's works by the time he was fifteen and remained a great admirer throughout his life. In 1931, Einstein wrote:

John Dalton, who was often compared to Newton, conducted experiments that expanded on Newton's work on color and light.

Fortunate Newton, happy childhood of science! . . . In one person he combined the experimenter, the theorist, the mechanic and, not least, the artist in exposition. He stands before us strong, certain, and alone. . . . Newton's discoveries have passed into the stock of accepted knowledge.[98]

Seeking Answers

The questions Newton devoted his life to studying were deceptively simple. Newton looked around him and wondered, What is light? What force keeps us tied to the earth, what holds the moon in its orbit, and what binds the universe together? These simple questions had very profound answers, and in answering them, Newton developed the basic ideas that underlie modern science. His work is still vital and scientists are still struggling to find more complete answers to the questions he posed. Nobel prize-winning astrophysicist Subrahmanyan Chandrasekhar of the University of Chicago said he was "astonished at the originality, the . . . elegance" of Newton's work. "Every time I looked at what Newton did, I felt like a schoolboy admonished by his master."[99]

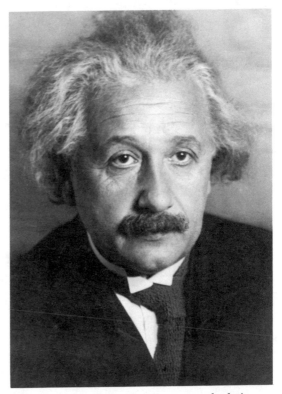

Albert Einstein, Newton's most renowned admirer. Even though his ideas would replace many of Newton's, Einstein remained an avid admirer of his famous predecessor.

And as scientists continue to probe the mysteries of gravity or probe the dark reaches of space, they will be taking up Newton's work once again and continuing in the footsteps of the master.

Notes

Introduction: A Sharper Eye

1. I. Bernard Cohen, *Revolution in Science.* Boston: Belknap Press of Harvard University Press, 1985.

Chapter 1: The Birth of a Genius

2. Gale E. Christianson, *In the Presence of the Creator.* New York: The Free Press, 1984.
3. Christianson, *In the Presence of the Creator.*
4. Christianson, *In the Presence of the Creator.*
5. John William Navin Sullivan, *Isaac Newton 1642-1727.* New York: The Macmillan Company, 1938.
6. Frank E. Manuel, *A Portrait of Isaac Newton.* New York: Da Capo Press, Inc., 1968.
7. Louis Trenchard More, *Isaac Newton, A Biography.* New York: Charles Scribner's Sons, 1934.
8. Christianson, *In the Presence of the Creator.*
9. Henry Thomas and Dana Lee Thomas, *Living Biographies of Great Scientists.* New York: Doubleday & Company, 1959.
10. More, *Isaac Newton, A Biography.*
11. Christianson, *In the Presence of the Creator.*

Chapter 2: The Seeds of Genius

12. Christianson, *In the Presence of the Creator.*
13. Derek T. Whiteside, ed., *Mathematical Papers of Newton.* Cambridge: Cambridge University Press, 1967.
14. Manuel, *A Portrait of Isaac Newton.*
15. Christianson, *In the Presence of the Creator.*
16. Christianson, *In the Presence of the Creator.*
17. Sullivan, *Isaac Newton 1642-1727.*
18. Jack Vrooman, *René Descartes, A Biography.* New York: G.P. Putnam's Sons, 1970.
19. Manuel, *A Portrait of Isaac Newton.*
20. Manuel, *A Portrait of Isaac Newton.*

Chapter 3: Recognition

21. More, *Isaac Newton, A Biography.*
22. Christianson, *In the Presence of the Creator.*
23. Christianson, *In the Presence of the Creator.*
24. Christianson, *In the Presence of the Creator.*
25. More, *Isaac Newton, A Biography.*
26. Daniel Boorstin, *The Discoverers.* New York: Random House, 1983.
27. More, *Isaac Newton, A Biography.*
28. Sullivan, *Isaac Newton 1642-1727.*
29. More, *Isaac Newton, A Biography.*
30. More, *Isaac Newton, A Biography.*
31. Christianson, *In the Presence of the Creator.*
32. Sullivan, *Isaac Newton 1642-1727.*
33. Jean-Pierre Maury, *Newton, the Father of Modern Astronomy.* New York: Harry N. Abrams, Inc., Publishers, 1992.
34. Maury, *Newton, the Father of Modern Astronomy.*

Chapter 4: Years of Discovery and Challenge

35. Sullivan, *Isaac Newton 1642-1727.*
36. Christianson, *In the Presence of the Creator.*
37. Christianson, *In the Presence of the Creator.*
38. Sullivan, *Isaac Newton 1642-1727.*
39. More, *Isaac Newton, A Biography.*
40. Christianson, *In the Presence of the Creator.*
41. Christianson, *In the Presence of the Creator.*
42. Christianson, *In the Presence of the Creator.*
43. More, *Isaac Newton, A Biography.*
44. Sullivan, *Isaac Newton 1642-1727.*
45. Sullivan, *Isaac Newton 1642-1727.*
46. More, *Isaac Newton, A Biography.*
47. Sullivan, *Isaac Newton 1642-1727.*
48. Sullivan, *Isaac Newton 1642-1727.*
49. Rutherford Aris, H. Ted Davis, and Roger

H. Stuewer, eds., *Spring of Scientific Creativity.* Minneapolis: University of Minnesota Press, 1983.

50. More, *Isaac Newton, A Biography.*

51. More, *Isaac Newton, A Biography.*

52. Christianson, *In the Presence of the Creator.*

53. Thomas and Thomas, *Living Biographies of Great Scientists.*

54. Thomas and Thomas, *Living Biographies of Great Scientists.*

55. Christianson, *In the Presence of the Creator.*

56. Thomas and Thomas, *Living Biographies of Great Scientists.*

Chapter 5: The Price of Genius

57. Christianson, *In the Presence of the Creator.*

58. Christianson, *In the Presence of the Creator.*

59. Christianson, *In the Presence of the Creator.*

60. Christianson, *In the Presence of the Creator.*

61. Christianson, *In the Presence of the Creator.*

62. Christianson, *In the Presence of the Creator.*

63. Sullivan, *Isaac Newton 1642-1727.*

64. Sullivan, *Isaac Newton 1642-1727.*

65. Christianson, *In the Presence of the Creator.*

66. Christianson, *In the Presence of the Creator.*

67. Christianson, *In the Presence of the Creator.*

68. More, *Isaac Newton, A Biography.*

69. More, *Isaac Newton, A Biography.*

70. More, *Isaac Newton, A Biography.*

71. H.D. Anthony, *Sir Isaac Newton.* London: Abelard-Schuman Limited, 1960.

72. More, *Isaac Newton, A Biography.*

73. Anthony, *Sir Isaac Newton.*

74. Manuel, *A Portrait of Isaac Newton.*

75. Manuel, *A Portrait of Isaac Newton.*

76. Manuel, *A Portrait of Isaac Newton.*

77. Anthony, *Sir Isaac Newton.*

78. I. Bernard Cohen, *Album of Science.* New York: Charles Scribner's Sons, 1980.

79. More, *Isaac Newton, A Biography.*

Chapter 6: The Final Years

80. Christianson, *In the Presence of the Creator.*

81. Anthony, *Sir Isaac Newton.*

82. Manuel, *A Portrait of Isaac Newton.*

83. Christianson, *In the Presence of the Creator.*

84. Christianson, *In the Presence of the Creator.*

85. More, *Isaac Newton, A Biography.*

86. Manuel, *A Portrait of Isaac Newton.*

87. Christianson, *In the Presence of the Creator.*

88. Sullivan, *Isaac Newton 1642-1727.*

Chapter 7: A Lasting Influence

89. James Burke, *The Day the Universe Changed.* Boston: Little, Brown and Company, 1985.

90. John Fauvel, Raymond Flood, Michael Shortland, and Robin Wilson, eds., *Let Newton Be!* New York: Oxford University Press, 1988.

91. Anthony, *Sir Isaac Newton.*

92. Fauvel, Flood, Shortland, and Wilson, eds., *Let Newton Be!*

93. Fauvel, Flood, Shortland, and Wilson, eds., *Let Newton Be!*

94. Fauvel, Flood, Shortland, and Wilson, eds., *Let Newton Be!*

95. More, *Isaac Newton, A Biography.*

96. More, *Isaac Newton, A Biography.*

97. Thomas and Thomas, *Living Biographies of Great Scientists.*

98. Fauvel, Flood, Shortland, and Wilson, eds., *Let Newton Be!*

99. Stefi Weisburd, "Celebrating Newton," *Science News,* July 4, 1987.

For Further Reading

William Bixby, *The Universe of Galileo and Newton*. New York: American Heritage, 1964. Scientific history that explores the theories of the two scientists within the context of their societies.

Phillippe de Cotardiere, *Astronomy*. New York: Facts On File, 1987. Scientific overview of the field of astronomy.

C.C. Gillispie, ed., *Dictionary of Scientific Biography*. New York: Charles Scribner's Sons, 1980. Scientific biography that gives a brief overview of some of history's greatest scientists.

Deborah Hitzeroth, *Telescopes: Searching the Heavens*. San Diego: Lucent Books, 1991. Science history with a focus on how technology has impacted the world.

Deborah Hitzeroth and Sharon Heerboth, *The Importance of Galileo Galilei*. San Diego: Lucent Books, 1992. Biography exploring the life of scientist Galileo Galilei and his impact on world development.

Frank E. Manuel, *Isaac Newton*. Cambridge, MA: Harvard University Press, 1963. Scientific biography that uses quotes and primary-source quotations to explore Newton's life.

Richard S. Westfall, *Never at Rest: A Biography of Isaac Newton*. New York: Cambridge University Press, 1981. Biography of Isaac Newton and his major contributions to the field of science.

Works Consulted

H.D. Anthony, *Sir Isaac Newton*. London: Abelard-Schuman Limited, 1960. Portrays the life and work of Newton within the framework of contemporary history. Contains an overview of Newton's greatest works as well as their impact on society.

Rutherford Aris, H. Ted Davis, and Roger H. Stuewer, eds., *Spring of Scientific Creativity*. Minneapolis: University of Minnesota Press, 1983. A series of essays exploring the creative process behind scientific discoveries and examining the lives of great scientists in history.

Daniel J. Boorstin, *The Discoverers*. New York: Random House, 1983. World history with a focus on the discoveries that aided human progress.

James Burke, *The Day the Universe Changed*. Boston: Little, Brown and Company, 1985. Scientific history with an emphasis on the theories that had the most profound effects on world history.

Gale E. Christianson, *In the Presence of the Creator*. New York: The Free Press, 1984. Christianson draws on Newton's correspondence and papers to paint a picture of his life in a seventeenth-century context.

John Fauvel, Raymond Flood, Michael Shortland, and Robin Wilson, eds., *Let Newton Be!* New York: Oxford University Press, 1988. A series of essays exploring the importance of Newton's life and his scientific achievements.

Judy Jones and William Wilson, *An Incomplete Education*. New York: Ballantine, 1987. History of art, economics, philosophy, religion, and science.

Aaron B. Lerner, *Einstein & Newton*. Minneapolis: Lerner Publications Company, 1973. Book compares the lives of Albert Einstein and Sir Isaac Newton. Focuses on how a person's background and experience influence his potential for achievement.

Frank E. Manuel, *A Portrait of Isaac Newton*. New York: Da Capo Press, Inc., 1968. A study of Newton's complex character through his letters and journals.

Jean-Pierre Maury, *Newton, the Father of Modern Astronomy*. New York: Harry N. Abrams, Inc., 1992. Gives an overview of Newton's involvement in the history of astronomy. Also contains brief synopsis of the works of other astronomers of Newton's period.

Louis Trenchard More, *Isaac Newton, a Biography*. New York: Charles Scribner's Sons, 1934. Draws heavily on Newton's primary papers to give a portrait of the scientist. Published on the bicentenary of Newton's death.

Robert S. Richardson, *The Star Lovers*. New York: The Macmillan Company, 1967. The author looks at the lives of sixteen famous astronomers, beginning with Tycho Brahe in the sixteenth century and ending with the life of Walter Baade, born in 1893. Richardson gives a general account of each scientist's career as well as an overview of their contributions to the world of astronomy.

John William Navin Sullivan, *Isaac Newton 1642-1727*. New York: The Macmillan

Company, 1938. A general biography of Newton including excerpts from Newton's correspondence and publications.

Henry Thomas and Dana Lee Thomas, *Living Biographies of Great Scientists*. New York: Doubleday & Company, 1959. Contains a brief biography of twenty scientists, beginning with the ancient Greek philosopher Archimedes and ending with Albert Einstein.

Stefi Weisburd, "Celebrating Newton," *Science News*, July 4, 1987. Author looks at the legacy of Isaac Newton three hundred years after the publication of the *Principia*.

Derek T. Whiteside, ed., *Mathematical Papers of Newton*. Cambridge: Cambridge University Press, 1967. A compilation of Newton's mathematical theories.

Index

Picture Credits

Cover photo by Historical Pictures/Stock Montage

Ann Ronan at Image Select, 34, 63, 64, 69 (bottom), 75 (both)

The Bettmann Archive, 14, 15, 23, 31, 42, 50 (bottom), 54, 55, 58, 71, 72 (bottom), 74, 79, 84

Culver Pictures, 9, 41

Giraudon/Art Resource, NY, 35

Historical Pictures/Stock Montage, 11, 12, 20, 28, 33, 37, 48, 50 (top), 62, 65, 66

Hulton-Deutsch, 10, 13, 17, 24, 38, 68, 72 (top), 78, 81, 83

Library of Congress, 22 (both), 26, 27, 30, 39, 45, 46, 47, 80, 85

NASA, 25, 51

National Library of Medicine, 57

North Wind Picture Archives, 69 (top), 77

University of California, Lawrence Berkeley Laboratory, 29

UPI/Bettmann, 19

Victoria & Albert Museum, London/Art Resource, NY, 60

About the Authors

Sisters Deborah Hitzeroth and Sharon Leon write as a team. Hitzeroth lives in Virginia and Leon lives in Texas. Hitzeroth's writing background includes a bachelor's degree in journalism from the University of Missouri and four years of newspaper experience. She has worked as a section editor on a daily paper and as a freelance writer for magazines in New York and Texas. This is her sixth book.

Leon has a bachelor's degree from the University of Missouri and an associate's degree from Texas State Technical Institute. She has written in-house technical and educational materials. This is her third book.